GONE TO RUSSIA TO FIGHT

THE RAF IN SOUTH RUSSIA 1918-1920

GONE TO RUSSIA TO FIGHT

THE RAF IN SOUTH RUSSIA 1918-1920

JOHN T. SMITH

AMBERLEY

First published 2010

Amberley Publishing Plc
Cirencester Road, Chalford,
Stroud, Gloucestershire, GL6 8PE

www.amberley-books.com

British Library Cataloguing in Publication Data.
A catalogue record for this book is available from the British Library.

ISBN 978 1 84868 891 9

Typeset in 10pt on 12pt Sabon.
Typesetting and Origination by FONTHILLDESIGN.
Printed in the UK.

CONTENTS

By the same author:

Rolling Thunder

The Linebacker Raids

Detail of picture on p. 113.

MAPS

ACKNOWLEDGEMENTS

Most of the information about the RAF in south Russia is contained in the National Archives at Kew. The staff at Kew are never less than helpful and courteous. The people at the RAF Museum, Hendon, London are real enthusiasts and I thank them for the help they gave me. Other sources consulted were:

The Tank Museum at Bovington, Dorset
The Army Museum at Chelsea, London
The British Library, London
The Maritime Museum at Greenwich, London
The Canadian National Archives
The Canadian Armed Forces Museum
The US National Archives

The photographs are from the Canadian Archives and the Canadian Armed Forces Museum. I would like to thank David Rogers, who read the manuscript. Any mistakes are all mine.

The quality of some of the photographs is poor but they have been included because they were the best available.

A painting by Mick Davison depicting the incident on 30 July 1919 over the
Volga River port of Tcherni-Yar, for which Captain W. F. Anderson and Lieutenant
Mitchell were both awarded the DSO. Captain Anderson was the pilot of a DH9
that was hit by ground fire in the fuel tank, and Lieutenant Mitchell was forced to
climb out onto the wing to block the leaking fuel with his thumb. Another DH9
in Anderson's flight was also hit by machine gun fire and forced to land behind
enemy lines. Anderson landed close by and picked up Captain Elliot and Lieutenant
Laidlaw. With Mitchell still on the wing, Anderson managed to take off, just before
an enemy cavalry patrol arrived, and fly them back to base.

INTRODUCTION

Very little has been written about the RAF in south Russia and much of what has been written has been inaccurate. Several myths have been accepted as truths and written into the histories. This book is an attempt to set the record straight by going back, where possible, to the primary sources.

The first wave of RAF personnel sent to south Russia was not given any choice in the matter. Most of the men had volunteered or been conscripted to fight in the First World War against Germany, Austria, and Turkey. They found themselves, after the end of the 'real' war, fighting in the middle of Russia in a civil war they knew little of and cared even less about. But they overcame enormous difficulties and made a substantial contribution to General Denikin's temporary successes.

The second wave of RAF people sent to south Russia comprised volunteers. These included many experienced flyers from the Western Front in France and from the Middle East. Many of them had found great difficulty in settling down to peace and relished the chance of further combat in Russia. Together with those people from the first wave who decided to stay, these later volunteers formed an elite group who played a leading part in the civil war, out of all proportion to their limited numbers. The exploits, in difficult circumstances, of the RAF in south Russia deserve to be better remembered.

The RAF men seem to have liked and respected the Russians individually, but did not understand the Russian way of doing things. The massive corruption in Denikin's Army, whereby large amounts of money and equipment simply vanished, forced the British to lose faith in the eventual victory of the White Armies.

With the success of the Red Army and the creation of the Soviet Union, there seems to have been a conscious effort by the British authorities to play down or forget the part that Britain played in the efforts to crush the nascent communist state. But the RAF achieved amazing things and deserve to have the truth told about their deeds in south Russia.

In late 1919, the RAF changed from Army ranks to RAF ranks. Army ranks have been used throughout this book to avoid confusion.

CHAPTER ONE

THE RUSSIAN CIVIL WAR

The Russian Civil War was one of the major wars of the twentieth century. It lasted between 1917 and 1926, but the main fighting took place between 1918 and 1920. Thirteen million Russians died during the course of the war. Most of these died of starvation, privation, and pestilence rather than as a result of direct military action. As in all civil wars, there were acts of extreme atrocity on both sides. In fact, it is hard to speak of two sides, as what are called the White Armies were never united in any common cause and covered all factions of political thought and ethnic backgrounds. Some sections of the anti-Bolshevik forces spent more time fighting each other than the Red Army. Also involved were the troops of up to fourteen foreign countries, including Britain, France, Japan, America, Greece, and Rumania. At the time of the Civil War, Russia was the largest country in the world and the fighting extended from the Arctic in the north to the deserts in the south and from Poland in the west to Vladivostok in the east.

The massive destruction caused by the First World War had triggered unrest among the revolutionary forces that had existed in Russian society for many years. In February 1917, the first Revolution deposed the Tsar and created the Kerensky government. But the decision to stay in the war allowed the more extreme revolutionary forces to continue to press for a more radical government. What was left of the Imperial Army began to fade away from the front line as a consequence of both these revolutionary pressures and military exhaustion. The October Revolution (November in the new calendar) created what became the Soviet government. This new government found itself beset by opponents on all sides.

As the Bolsheviks had played a large part in destroying the Imperial Army, they found themselves with few forces to fight the gathering enemies they faced. Trotsky is usually credited with creating the Red Army, and there is no doubt that he played a considerable role. Rather than use what remained of the Tsar's Army, the first reaction was to build a new Army based on the Red Guards. These were originally armed factory workers, who elected their commanders and discussed every action before carrying it out. As the new state came under threat, large numbers volunteered to join the new Army and, later still, millions were conscripted. When revolutionary fervour was found to be no substitute for military experience, Trotsky was forced to employ thousands of ex-Tsarist officers as 'military specialists'. But he placed a party commissar alongside each officer. As the fighting continued, the Red Army slowly became a conventional Army, with no pretence of electing officers or discussions of any decisions. Party orders were enforced with an iron hand, and thousands of Red Army soldiers were killed to enforce discipline.

Many of the minorities in the former Russian Empire took the Bolshevik rhetoric at face value and tried to create their own independent states. These included the Cossack homelands, Poland, Finland, Latvia, Estonia, Lithuania, Georgia, Azerbaijan, Armenia, Transcaucasia, and areas of Siberia. The Red Army fought against all of these breakaway states, sometimes successfully and sometimes not.

In the north, around Murmansk and Archangel, there were enormous stocks of arms and munitions that had been sent to Russia by the Allies. British, French, and American troops were sent to this region originally to keep these supplies out of the hands of the Germans, and then to deny them to the Bolshevik government. The Allies advanced south towards St Petersburg, but were blocked by Soviet forces and by the desolate terrain. After two miserable years in the frozen north, the last Allied troops left in 1919.

The White forces in north-western Russia were concentrated along the eastern shore of the Baltic. Commanding this force was General Yudenitch. At various times, this group was supported by the Germans and, later, by the Allies. A British squadron in the Baltic, under the command of Admiral Walter Cowan, gave every assistance to the White forces, and British supplies were sent through the port at Riga. Several attempts were made to capture St Petersburg but, although they came close, this was never achieved. By November 1919, the Bolsheviks had destroyed this Army and the remnants were forced back into Estonia, where they were disbanded in January 1920.

One of the most amazing stories of the Russian Civil War was that of the Czech Legion. The Legion had been a corps in the Imperial Russian Army, formed from Austro-Hungarian prisoners who were willing to fight for a Czech homeland to be created after the war. When the Imperial Army collapsed and the Soviet government reached an agreement with the Germans, the Legion was practically the only part of the Russian Army to remain an organised, disciplined force. With the end of the First World War in the east, the Legion demanded to be transported to Vladivostok and then to France so that it could continue to fight. By May 1918, the Legion had grown, with the release of more prisoners by the Russians, to around 50,000 strong. As the Legion began to move east towards Vladivostok, an incident occurred with a trainload of released Austrian POWs, and the Legion began to fight the Red Army. After several days, it controlled nearly 5,000 miles of the Trans-Siberian Railway. The Czechs, who had reached Vladivostok, now began to move back westward towards Moscow.

To support the Czech Legion and to protect the large amount of supplies the Allies had delivered to the Russians in Vladivostok before the Russians had surrendered, the Allies (including the French, British, Americans, and Japanese) landed troops in Vladivostok. The Czechs had joined forces with the anti-Bolshevik Army operating around the Omsk and Samara areas to push back the Red forces. A White Russian government was formed around these forces, controlled by Admiral Kolchak. This became the Supreme Government, and all the other major anti-Bolshevik forces gave nominal allegiance to Kolchak. But, in practical terms, this allegiance did not have any real meaning. In late 1918 and early 1919, Admiral Kolchak's forces began to advance towards Moscow, but the Red Army rallied and by the middle of 1919 forced them back east of the Urals. Czech soldiers handed Admiral Kolchak over to the Reds in January 1920. What was left of the Czech Legion finally left Vladivostok in 1920, bound for the new homeland of Czechoslovakia, which had been created by the Versailles Peace Conference. As the Red Army advanced through Siberia, the Allied forces began to leave, the last being the Japanese in 1922.

Supported by the Germans, both Finland and Poland successfully broke away from Russian control. Both these countries fought long-drawn-out campaigns to maintain their independence. Poland developed ideas of recreating the Polish Empire that stretched from the Baltic to the Black Sea, and at one point in 1920 it seemed that this was a possibility, but once again the Red Army fought back and an armistice was signed. The Germans had occupied the Ukraine in 1917-18, and the Brest-Litovsk Treaty recognised the new state. But when the Germans left, the Ukraine descended into chaos. From this chaos a nationalist government took control, commanded by Simon Petlyura. A strong Bolshevik movement controlled some areas of the country, and disparate nationalist factions also fought each other. The White Russian forces of General Denikin captured a large section of the country in late 1919. The Red Army finally took control of the Ukraine in 1920.

Various Cossack hosts fought against the Red Army. These included the Don Cossacks, the Kuban Cossacks, the Terek Cossacks, the Astrakhan

Cossacks, the Ural Cossacks, and the Siberian Cossacks. They all hoped to create their own homelands from the remains of the Russian Empire. It was correctly thought that the Soviet government would end the special rules relating to the Cossack areas that had in the past allowed them a limited amount of self-government. A more detailed description of the Civil War in south Russia will be given in Chapter Three.

Starting from practically nothing, the Red Army managed to defeat all these different enemies. There was little or no co-ordination between the White forces, and the Red Army was able to defeat them in detail. The central area of Russia around Moscow and St Petersburg remained in the hands of the Bolsheviks throughout the war. This was the area containing most of the industry and most of the Imperial Army's arms dumps, plus a large part of the population. Few of the original Bolshevik leaders had any military experience, or experience of organising anything larger than a party meeting, but they managed to create an Army from scratch and to keep the county running in the face of enormous difficulties.

During the course of the Civil War, the political base, culture, and civilisation of large parts of Russia collapsed. Into this country, in a state of total change, were sent small numbers of RAF forces in a vain attempt to determine the outcome of the conflict.

CHAPTER TWO

DUNSTERFORCE

The Bolshevik revolution in late 1917 had effectively taken Russia out of the First World War. In the chaos that followed, many of the smaller provinces that made up the Russian Empire declared themselves independent. This occurred in the south Caucasus, where Georgia, Armenia, and Azerbaijan allied themselves as the TransCaucasian Commissariat, even though there was no love lost between these three breakaway states. In March 1918, the Russians signed the Brest-Litovsk Treaty with Germany and Turkey. As part of this treaty, Georgia, Armenia, and Azerbaijan were given to the Turks.

Not surprisingly, the TransCaucasian government refused to accept this settlement and a Turkish Army began to advance towards the oil-fields at Baku. After less than a month, the TransCaucasian Commissariat broke up. The Georgians placed themselves under German protection in order to keep out the Turks. Most of Armenia was occupied by the advancing Turkish Army, as was most of Azerbaijan. The oil town of Baku, in Azerbaijan, with a large industrial work-force, had created a Bolshevik Soviet to run the area around the town.

Many of the Moslem Azerbaijanis supported the Turks. In late March, the Soviet forces and the Armenians carried out a massacre of as many as 12,000 Azerbaijanis in Baku. The Turkish advance was extremely slow, as most of their effort was still directed against the British forces in Palestine and Mesopotamia. But, finally, the Turkish forces reached the peninsula on which Baku is situated. On 30 July, the Soviet was dissolved and replaced by the Armenian-controlled Centro-Caspian Dictatorship. One of the first acts of the new government in Baku was to invite the British to help in the defence of the town.

A small party of British forces had been waiting in north Persia to be invited into Baku. This was under the command of Major General Lionel Dunsterville. Composed mainly of Army officers, this small force had set

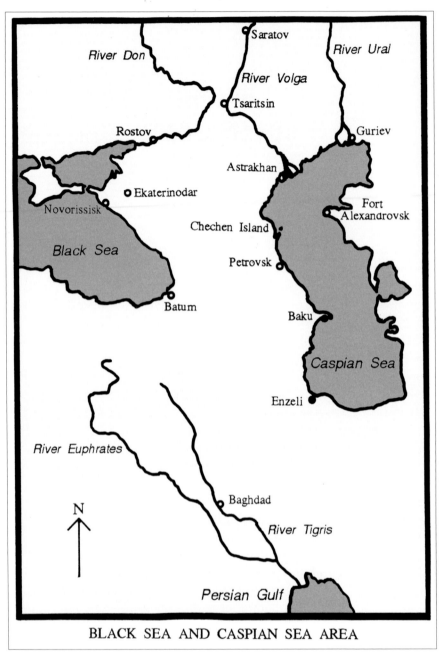

BLACK SEA AND CASPIAN SEA AREA

The area of operations for Dunsterforce.

Left: Commodore David Norris. Right: General Lionel Dunsterville.

out from Baghdad with forty-one Ford model T cars and vans to drive the 700 miles north-east to the Caspian Sea. After many adventures, this group was waiting in the port of Enzeli on the south Caspian shore. Commodore David Norris and twenty-two ratings were the Naval element of this force.

The British aims were to keep the oil from Baku out of the hands of the Germans and the Turks. Also, the main rail line from Moscow to the area north of British India ran down through the Caucasus (the route continued across the Caspian by ship, and then from Krasnovodsk on the eastern shore to Afghanistan): it was the aim of the British to prevent the spread of Bolshevism to India by controlling the Caspian link. Commodore Norris had left Baghdad on 27 July 1918 with one four-inch gun and two twelve-pounders. Very little was known of the conditions on the Caspian and no charts were available, as no Royal Navy ships had ever sailed on it. It was not even known if suitable merchant ships would be available to mount the guns on.

The route from Baghdad to Enzeli ran for 700 miles of mule and camel tracks. Most of the way was through high mountainous regions. The Ford vans could only carry just enough fuel to reach Enzeli. On 5 August, Norris arrived at Enzeli and had his first sight of the Caspian. Money was paid by the British to the local authorities at Enzeli to allow them to use the port. General Dunsterville was anxious to obtain the shipping needed to move his forces to Baku. All the available Naval personnel and guns from the Far East were beginning to make the long trek overland to the Caspian Sea. Army reinforcements also began to move forward from Baghdad to reinforce General Dunsterville.

The first ship chartered by the Navy was the SS *President Kruger*. On 16 August 1918, General Dunsterville and his staff, along with Commodore Norris, set sail for Baku in the *Kruger*, arriving the following day. Baku was the largest port on the Caspian, and the population had increased with the influx of people to work in the oil industry. Parts of the town were made up of large modern buildings, but other parts were only shacks separated by cart tracks. To the west of the town, was a large oil-field and refinery. The population was a mix of Armenian, Russian, and Azerbaijani.

Most of the fighting against the Turks was being done by Armenian troops. As soon as even a small number of British troops arrived, the Armenians considered that they had done enough fighting and many of the troops returned to Baku. But General Dunsterville pointed out that the British could only supply limited numbers of troops, and the intention was only to provide support for the Armenians. Two more ships, the SS *Kursk* and the SS *Abo*, were taken over by the British. As the Army and Navy reinforcement arrived in Enzeli, they were shipped across the Caspian to

The seafront at Baku.

Baku. Dunsterville only had around 1,200 British troops to support 8,000 Armenian troops against the 14,000-strong Turkish forces. Also, most of the surviving Azerbaijanis, after the massacre in Baku, were now working for the Turks.

The Turks launched a major attack towards Baku on 26 August. British forces were driven back from a defensive position called the Mud Volcano. Two local battalions had been ordered forward to support the British troops but had never appeared at the front. This had given General Dunsterville extreme misgivings about the vulnerability of the British. Another major attack was launched on 31 August and again the British were forced back. The numbers of British casualties continued to rise. During this action, General Dunsterville witnessed an entire Russian battalion leave the front and flee.

General Dunsterville called all the different groups in Baku to the Hotel Europa on 1 September. He stated that unless they were prepared to fight, then no power on earth could save them from the Turks. All the parties involved agreed that things would change. The Turks did not carry out any more advances for the next two weeks.

The air support for the British force was to be provided by aircraft from 72 Squadron. This squadron was nominally based at Baghdad but had been broken into separate flights. A Flight was based at Samara and equipped with DH4s and SE5As. C Flight was at Marjiana with Bristol monoplanes. B Flight had been operating with the Army in north Persia against local insurgents known colloquially as the Jungalies. The squadron diary reads:

> The bombing raids that followed on the Jungalies so completely demoralised them, that the mere sight of Aeroplanes put them to flight, and our troops were able to occupy Resht.[1]

B Flight was stationed on the airfield at Hamadan in north Persia. They were equipped with Martinsyde G.102 Elephants, large single-seat reconnaissance aircraft. Lieutenant A. A. Cullen, who was part of A Flight but also flew the Martinsyde, described the aircraft:

> Jumbo Martinsyde, a big rather clumsy single seater, with a 150 HP Beardmore engine, originally designed for long reconnaissance flights.[2]

Two Martinsydes were sent from Hamadan to support the British forces in Baku. On 15 August 1918, Lieutenants M. C. Mackay and R. P. P. Pope were told to prepare their aircraft for the trip to Baku. On 18 August, the aircraft were flown to Enzeli, where they were dismantled and stripped to enable them to be carried on a ship. The Turks held most of the coast and it was not thought a good idea to fly the aircraft direct. The airfield at Baku was four miles outside the town. After they were unloaded onto the docks, the aircraft were taken to the airfield by truck. By 25 August, the aircraft had been reassembled and a two-hour test flight using local petrol was successfully carried out.

False reports were received that German fighter aircraft were operating with the Turks at Baku. To counter this threat, it was decided to send three of A Flight's SE5As to Baku. The aircraft were sent forward from Baghdad. The pilots were Lieutenants A. A. Cullen, Pitt, and Cannel. On 19 August, Lieutenant Cullen crashed his SE5A while landing at an airfield at Kermanshah. The next day, he was forced to follow the other two SE5As by car to Hamadan. On 21 August, Lieutenant Cannel crashed his SE5A while taking off from Hamadan. Later in the month, Lieutenant Cullen made a forced landing behind Turkish lines while carrying out a reconnaissance flight and was taken prisoner. The plan to send the SE5As to Baku was abandoned.

General Dunsterville only had the two Martinsydes and two Russian flying boats operating from the harbour at Baku as effective aircraft. There were other Russian aircraft operating from the airfield outside the town, but they did not provide effective support. The squadron diary states:

On the 27th August Major Boyd, visited Baku with Captain Fuller and in his report on Aviation generally, remarked on the little enterprise by the Russian Pilots, and as they did not appear to understand the first rudiments of war flying, we were prepared not to receive much support from them.[3]

General Dunsterville did what he could with the limited forces at his command. But the expedition was doomed from the start.

The two Martinsydes, during the twenty-one days they were flying in Baku, carried out reconnaissances, bombing, and leaflet dropping. Rumours of German-flown fighter aircraft proved to be false and no aerial opposition was encountered. An attempt was made to carry out spotting for the Russian artillery gunners, but the Martinsydes were not equipped with radio. A system of dropping information in message bags was tried, but this did not work very well.

In the harbour at Baku was the Centro-Caspian Flotilla, comprising a number of armed ships. This naval force was nominally supporting the political leadership on the shore, but was in reality only maintaining its own position. The Flotilla was determined to stop the British from arming any more ships, as this would threaten their situation of superiority on the Caspian. After heavy fighting, the Turks closed in on the port and General Dunsterville told the Armenians that if they could not hold the Turks off the British would have to evacuate.

The RAF personnel were forced to evacuate on 4 September, along with the rest of the Army. Lieutenant Mackay wrote the report on the evacuation. It is worth quoting the report in full:

About an hour before daybreak on the 14th September, the Turks attacked the Allied lines West of Baku. Their main attack was concentrated on Wolf's Gap – a large break in the British Ridge – through which ran a road. At dawn Lieutenant Mackay flew over this sector of the line and observed troops on the British ridge. Owing to cloud and mist at 1,000 ft. the identification of these troops was difficult, and to avoid any mistake the pilot flew farther West to the Turkish ridge where enemy reserves were seen halted on the Western slopes. Six drums from the Lewis were fired into these troops and a report taken back to HQ as to their whereabouts. During the morning Lieutenant Pope did two reconnaissances – the first of 30 minutes – the second of 55 minutes. During the first, three drums were fired on to troops on the British ridge, who had now been identified as Turks. Owing to the gas regulator key falling away from his gun, Lieutenant Pope returned to the aerodrome – but the trouble having been remedied – again took off and crossed the Turkish lines.

Six drums were fired into Turkish troops who were now about half way between the old British ridge and Baku. Lieutenant Mackay crossed the enemy lines shortly after this and again fired six drums into the enemy reserves and the British ridge. The last three flights were carried out at 1,500 ft. Lieutenant Pope's machine had been unserviceable for a day or so previously and owing to shortage of mechanics and time required to be spent on the serviceable machine, only one machine flew on the 14th September. By 12.15pm on this day the machine was unfit to fly owing to hits from rifle and machine gun fire from the ground – and at 3pm orders were received from the G. O. C. British troops Baku, to destroy the two machines, their flying to Krasnovodsk, Lenkoran or Enzeli being out of the question. At 3.45pm the machines were burnt, the engine being rendered useless by revolver bullets and an axe. At 4.15pm Lieutenants Pope and Mackay left the aerodrome which was then under shell fire – taking away with them one (top) machine gun and three cameras. The RAF personnel was ordered to take one of the remaining machine guns and several drums of ammunition and join the British line which was then close to the northern end of the aerodrome. The third machine gun was smashed.

Bradley, with Lieutenants Pope and Mackay then left the aerodrome and proceeded to the Hotel Europa where all photographic chemicals and plates which were unable to be got away were destroyed. At 5pm Lieutenant Pope and Mackay were ordered to embark on a ship which got safely out of Baku at 8pm. The RAF personnel evacuated with the other British troops and were picked up at Enzeli. They had smashed up the last machine gun just before retiring to the quay at Baku. On the 18th instant a RAF tender arrived from Kasvan and took all RAF personnel back with it.[4]

The three British-commanded ships in the harbour at Baku were the *Abo*, the *Kursk* and the *Kruger*. During the afternoon of 14 August, the British forces began to pull back towards the harbour in an orderly fashion. The Centro-Caspian Flotilla in the harbour at Baku had stated that they would fire on any British ships that tried to leave. According to Navy records, the *Abo* left at 18.30 hours, carrying women, wounded, and various small parties (including the RAF officers). All the ships in the harbour were getting up steam and preparing to sail and nobody seems to have noticed the *Abo* leave. As the Army moved back to the port, the quay became choked with lorries, armoured cars, and mules, which all had to be abandoned. The *Kursk* left the harbour, carrying troops, around 23.00 hours. Some of the artillery was loaded onto the *Kruger*, and when it was clear that no one had been left behind, the ship pulled out of the harbour

HMS *Kruger*, General Dunsterville's flagship.

at 01.00 hours on 15 August. The Russian guard ship fired on the *Kruger* but no hits were achieved. All three ships arrived in Enzeli later the same day.

The Turks entered the town within hours of the British departure and in three days of massacre the Azerbaijanis killed 16,000 Armenians. After six weeks, the British were back in Enzeli where they had started. A number of ships had fled the fall of Baku and these were now in the harbour at Enzeli. The workshop facilities at Enzeli were limited, but work was started on the SS *Ventuir* with the intention of mounting on the vessel some of the guns that were now being delivered from Baghdad.

Commodore Norris decided to visit Krasnovodsk, on the eastern coast, to look for a better-equipped dockyard to use as a base. Krasnovodsk was controlled by an anti-Bolshevik committee and welcomed the British ship. There was a large railway workshop at Krasnovodsk and the British decided to use this as their fitting-out base. By the end of October, there were five armed British ships on the Caspian. These were the *Kruger, Ventuir, Asia, Alla Verdi,* and *Emile Nobel.* None of these were very large; they were all in poor condition and their guns were old-fashioned, but they did provide the basis of a British fleet on the Caspian.

In September, Commodore Norris had a serious accident and the command on the Caspian passed to Captain Washington. Also at this time, General Dunsterville was given a command in India and was replaced by General W. M. Thompson. Three more ships, the *Bibiat,* the *Slava,* and the *Zoro-Aster,* were in the process of being armed, thought ammunition remained in short supply. Eight 4.7-inch shells was one camel load for the

700-mile trip across north Persia from Baghdad. On 31 October, the Turks signed an armistice with the Allies.

The British naval squadron now began a series of cruises on the Caspian. Early in November, the five armed ships visited Petrovsk, north of Baku, and the *Asia* was sent to Guryev, a port on the river Ural. This was the headquarters of the Ural Cossacks, who were part of the White Russian forces fighting against the Reds. The main Bolshevik base on the Caspian was the port of Astrakhan, on the mouth of the Volga River. Using canals, it was possible to bring armed ships from the Baltic onto the Volga and down to the Caspian at Astrakhan. Using this supply route, the Bolsheviks were building up their forces in the north of the Caspian.

NOTES

[1] National Archives, 72 Squadron diary
[2] Cullen, A. A., unpublished memoir
[3] National Archives, 72 Squadron diary
[4] Ibid.

CHAPTER THREE

THE MILITARY SITUATION IN SOUTH RUSSIA

The original justification for British intervention in south Russia was the Anglo-French Agreement of 23 December 1917. When it became obvious that Russia would soon be out of the war against Germany, an agreement was reached between Britain and France. Under this agreement, the Allies were planning to continue an Eastern Front against Germany on Russian territory, with or without the support of the Bolshevik government. France was given responsibility for the area west of the river Don, and Britain was given the Caucasus and the area north and east of the Caspian. In truth, while the First World War continued, there was little that could be done against the German occupation of the Ukraine or Turkey's attempted occupation of the Caucasus. The Dunsterforce expedition had soon been driven out.

Earlier in 1917, the Kerensky government had asked the leader of the Army, General L. Kornilov, to move loyal Army units to St Petersburg to restore order. But as soon as Kornilov had started to move troops, Kerensky had lost his nerve and had him arrested for planning a military dictatorship. Kornilov was imprisoned, along with General Anton Denikin. They were held by military personnel, however, and were allowed to come and go as they pleased. The new head of the Army was General M. V. Alekseev. With the takeover of the Bolsheviks in the October 1917 Revolution (November in the new calendar), Alekseev fled to south Russia, thinking the Cossack regions in the south would be a centre of resistance to the Bolsheviks. In December 1917, he was joined by Generals Denikin and Kornilov, who had simply walked out of the prison in which they had been kept.

A small number of officers and men began to join Alekseev in the south to take part in the fight against the Bolsheviks. General Alekseev called this group the Volunteer Army. Most of the men joining Alekseev were officers, and some of the early units were made up entirely of officers. After

General Anton Denikin.

some disagreement, General Kornilov became the military commander and Alekseev the political chief. The Cossack hosts were as war-weary as the rest of Russian society and failed to rise against the Bolsheviks. Also, the numbers joining the Volunteer Army remained small and the promised finance failed to arrive.

During February 1918, Rostov was captured by detachments of the Red Guard sent out from Moscow. At this early stage of the Civil War, many sections of the population supported the Soviet government, not having yet suffered under Bolshevik rule. With the fall of Rostov, Alekseev and Kornilov led the Volunteer Army, now 4,000-strong, into the north Caucasus. To the Volunteers, this period became known as the 'Ice March'. During this time, massively superior numbers surrounded them on all sides as they marched across the frozen steppes. Kornilov, as the military commander, decided to attack Ekaterinodar, the Kuban Cossack capital, which was now the capital of the Kuban Soviet Republic, in order to give themselves a base for operations. The attack was started on 10 April 1918. During the fighting, Kornilov was killed by artillery fire when his command post in a farmhouse was hit. The command passed to General Denikin, who was forced to call off the attack on Ekaterinodar and retreat towards the Don territory.

Russia had been negotiating with Germany to end the fighting between them, but when these talks broke down during February 1918 the Germans again began to advance into Russia. What was left of the Russian Army melted away in front of the Germans. Large areas of eastern Europe were occupied, including the Ukraine. The Russians returned to the negotiations and signed the Brest-Litovsk peace on 3 March. As part of the settlement, the Germans were given a free hand in the Ukraine. On 8 May, they captured Rostov.

The Don Cossacks soon became tired of Soviet rule. In May 1918, a meeting of the Don Krug elected a new Ataman, General Peter Krasnov. The Red Guards only had a loose hold on the Don territory and were soon driven out. The region to the west of the territory held by the Don Cossacks was now occupied by the Germans, who supplied money and arms to the Cossacks. By the middle of June, the Don Cossacks had an Army of 40,000 operating against the Reds. The Red Army was still in its infancy and had few combat troops available to send to the south, forcing them to rely on local troops.

After they had reoccupied all their own territory, the Don Cossacks turned east to try to capture Tsaritsin. But, after months of fighting, they failed in their bid to take the city. Tsaritsin was a large, built-up industrial area with a substantial working-class population that had supported the Red takeover. Most of the Don Cossacks were cavalry, and they lacked

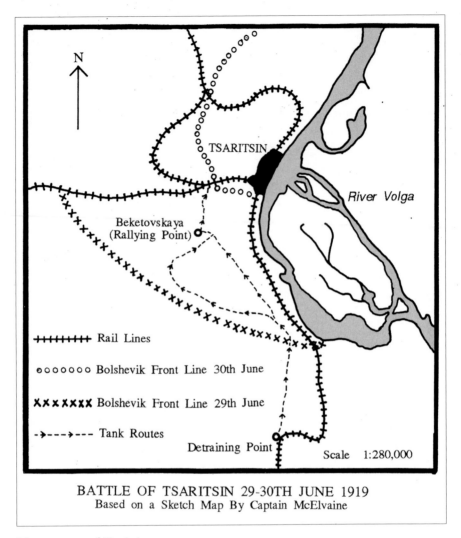

N

TSARITSIN

River Volga

Beketovskaya
(Rallying Point)

++++++++ Rail Lines

○○○○○○○ Bolshevik Front Line 30th June

XXXXXXX Bolshevik Front Line 29th June

-➤---➤--- Tank Routes

Detraining Point

Scale   1:280,000

BATTLE OF TSARITSIN 29-30TH JUNE 1919
Based on a Sketch Map By Captain McElvaine

The area around Tsaritsin.

General Baron Peter Wrangel.

the heavy forces needed to capture the trench lines around the city. In command in Tsaritsin during the summer of 1918 was Stalin, along with Vorishilov and Budenny in subordinate roles. Stalin clashed with Trotsky over the strategy in the south and over the use of ex-Tsarist officers in command positions and was finally recalled to Moscow.

The Volunteer Army was re-equipped with arms and munitions from Germany, acquired via the Don Cossacks. Volunteer Army policy had originally been to continue the war against Germany, but this does not seem to have stopped them taking German money and arms through the Cossacks. By June 1918, the Volunteer Army had grown to 9,000 and they again tried to capture the north Caucasus area from the Red government forces. On 18 August, they captured Ekaterinodar, the Kuban Cossack capital. Once they had been liberated, the Kuban Cossack leadership joined the Don Cossacks and the Volunteer Army in the fight against the Bolshevik forces.

The original Volunteer Army was an effective and disciplined force capable of defeating Red Army units of much larger numbers. General Denikin continued to advance eastward across the Caucasus, and the Red Army set up their new base at Piatigorsk on the main rail line to Tsaritsin. On 8 October 1918, General Alekseev died, leaving General Denikin as the undisputed leader of the Volunteer Army. The Don Cossacks were faced with the 8th and 9th Red Armies in the north and the 10th Army in Tsaritsin, but they continued to hold out against the increasing pressure. During August, General Peter Wrangel joined the Volunteer Army. Wrangel was forty years old and had been in the Army for seventeen years. He had risen to command a division in the First World War. When he arrived in Ekaterinodar, the Volunteer Army had grown in size to around 38,000 troops. Denikin, who knew Wrangel slightly, offered him command of a division in the Volunteer Army. Wrangel went on to become the most effective of the White generals.

The counter-revolution in the south was still a limited affair but the influx of huge amounts of Allied equipment, money, and men would transform the situation.

CHAPTER FOUR

DECEMBER 1918

The war with Turkey ended in October 1918 and the Armistice with Germany took effect on 11 November. This freed up access to the Black Sea. As part of the settlement, elements from the Allied forces occupied the fortifications along the Bosphorus. In late November, British ships from the Mediterranean fleet entered the Black Sea. This made the supplying of aid to the White forces in south Russia a practical proposition. Military supplies and men began to flow from bases around the eastern Mediterranean and Middle East into the quagmire of the Russian Civil War.

But the first British troops into south Russia were from the 14th Indian Army Division stationed in Iraq and Persia. On 17 November 1918, six days after the end of the First World War, Major General Thompson, who had replaced General Dunsterville, reoccupied Baku as the Turks withdrew. Escorted by the five armed ships under the command of Captain Washington, a convoy of seventeen merchant ships landed 2,000 British troops in the port at Baku. Another British Army force from Salonika occupied the port of Batum on the Black Sea. These two ports were connected by a rail line that ran along the southern line of the Caucasus Mountains, through the city of Tiflis. The supply problems for the British ships on the Caspian were reduced by this rail and sea link to the Mediterranean. The British occupation of the Transcaucasus region was intended to bring stability to the area of the largest oil-fields in the world, as well as to ease supply problems. It was also intended to disarm the area as the Turkish Army withdrew. But the number of British troops remained tiny in the context of the troubles in the region.

The British cabinet had taken the decision on 14 November to contact General Denikin and to provide him with military equipment and training. Major-General Frederick Poole had been recalled from the British forces

Tanks being delivered on the docks at Novorossisk.

in north Russia and it was decided to place him in command of the British
Military Mission to General Denikin. The capture of Novorossisk by
General Denikin's Volunteer Army, in late 1918, had given them an outlet
to the sea. Taking advantage of this, General Poole arrived in Novorossisk
in December 1918. The relations between General Denikin and the Don
Cossacks had never been particularly warm, although they had worked
together against the Red forces. But General Poole, with promises of
enormous amounts of British money and equipment, forced the Don
Cossacks under their Ataman General Peter Krasnov to place their forces
under the command of General Denikin.

To support the British Army and Navy forces in the area, the RAF began
to gather together units to send into south Russia. Number 17 Squadron
was stationed in Salonika and had taken part in the Bulgarian campaign.
In the middle of September, A Flight had its Armstrong Witworth aircraft
replaced by DH9s. Under the command of Captain A. D. Makins, A Flight
left Salonika on 31 December for the port of Batum.

Number 221 Squadron was also sent into south Russia. Stationed on
Mudros at the end of the war was Major John Oliver Andrews; writing in
the 1920s, he recalled the squadron's journey:

In November 1918, the Dardanelles being opened, a squadron of DH9s
was formed to proceed to S. Russia, with the idea of co-operating with
the Naval forces on the Caspian Sea, and with the Russian White Armies

operation under Denikin in the Caucasus. It was difficult to raise the necessary other rank personnel, due partly to the demoralisation and war weariness caused by the long sojourn in Mudros and Imbros ... In December, the unit, 221 Squadron, embarked in the S. S. Riviera, and proceeded via Constantinople and the Black Sea to Batum. The passage was uneventful, except for New Year's Eve spent at Constantinople with the R. N. R. and a spell of coal trimming and stoking undertaken by the squadron in the Black Sea, as the ship was short handed. It was universally agreed that coal shovelling in a ship's bunker is a poor way of making a livelihood.[1]

221 Squadron was to be part of 62 Wing, made up of 221 Squadron equipped with DH9s, and (later) DH9As; 266 Squadron equipped with Short 184 floatplanes; and
186 Squadron, to be equipped with Handley Page bombers. In the event, 186 Squadron never arrived.

Also stationed at Mudros at the end of the war was D. B. Knock, an armourer. In his diary, published in the 1930s, he described Major Andrews:

20/12/18 Remnants of Squadron re-formed as 221 Squadron RAF, with Major Andrews as CO. Things brushed up and discipline tightened up. Andrews won't stand any nonsense. A soldier from head to feet ... Have heard of his record in France with somewhere around 40 EA [enemy aircraft] to his credit [if aircraft driven down are included, Andrews' total was 24 EA]. Didn't get his DSO and MC for nothing. A pre-war soldier before RFC.[2]

D. B. Knock also related his experiences on the journey to Batum in his diary. He seems to have agreed with Andrews on the coal shovelling:

28/12/18 Orders to be ready to move early morning. Nobody knows really where, but rumours say Constantinople. Be great to see the city of Mosques. 'Planes, motor transport, ammunition, etc. all ready.
29/12/18 HQ staff and A Flight board HMS "Riviera" (seaplane carrier). At midnight. Sail at 2am. We enter Dardanelles at 8am ... Reach Constantinople at 9pm.
31/12/18 Not allowed ashore. Instead we help Navy stokers to coal from a collier moored alongside. Get as black as Hades drill slacks and tunic so black I trade them with a stoker for rum. He can wash them! Leave Bosphorus 8am and out into Black Sea. Wonderful sight that waterway is. 1919 breaks with a blue sea and the sight of HMS "Superb" at 10am

making from somewhere, probably Odessa. For Constantinople. [500 British marines had been landed in Sevastopol][3]

Another member of 221 Squadron was Lieutenant O. R. Gayford, an observer, who had earlier taken part in the bombing of Constantinople. He also described the journey:

By December 1918 the Squadron was completely equipped with Puma DH9s, [Major Andrews took one Bentley-engined Sopwith Camel with him for his own personal use] and was preparing to go up to the Caspian Sea for work with a naval squadron, which was on those inland waters. We left by Flights at intervals of about a fortnight in seaplane carriers via the Bosphorus to Batum on the Black Sea. Our aircraft were taken with engines installed and with undercarriages on, but wings and empennages dismantled.[4]

By the end of 1918, 221 Squadron had started the move into the Caucasus, but it was to be early 1919 before 266 Squadron, the seaplane squadron, joined them. The British Naval ships on the Caspian were active during December. On 8 December, two British ships, the *Zoro-Aster* and the *Alla Verdi*, were at anchor off Chechen Island, north of Baku, when three Bolshevik navy vessels were seen escorting three merchant ships. The Bolsheviks opened fire on the British ships, which left their moorings and chased the Red vessels. Hits were seen on the enemy ships, while three shells hit the *Zoro-Aster*. The Red vessels escaped, but in their first encounter the British ships had seen off a superior enemy with no losses. On 29 December, four of the British ships bombarded the Bolshevik base at Staro-Terechnaya. The British flotilla was now up to a strength of eight armed ships.

By the end of 1918, contact had been established with General Denikin to find out his military needs, and a small force of British troops had occupied the south Caucasus region.

NOTES

[1] National Archives, Andrews, J. O., War Experiences
[2] Knock, D. B., 'An Armourer's Diary', *Popular Flying*, May 1938, page 90
[3] Ibid.
[4] National Archives, Gayford, O. R., War Experiences

CHAPTER FIVE

JANUARY 1919

The military situation in the north Caucasus at the start of 1919 was that the Don Cossack Army was stretched thinly across the Don region. With the withdrawal of the German forces from the Ukraine, the Don Cossacks had lost their main source of weapons and support. General Krasnov, the Cossack leader, had identified himself too closely with the Germans, out of necessity, and his position was weakened with their removal. The Cossacks had reached the limits of their resources and the Red Southern Army Group had been built up to a force of 117,000 men, facing 40,000 Cossacks. Under this increased pressure from the north, the Cossacks were forced to retreat. The agreement giving General Denikin overall command was signed on 8 January by the Don Cossack leadership. The Armed Forces of South Russia was formed out of the Volunteer Army, the Don Cossacks, the Kuban Cossacks, and the Terek Cossacks.

The Volunteer Army was holding the area around Ekaterinodar and Novorossisk in the north-west of the Caucasus, facing the Red Caspian-Caucasus Army Group. This was made up of the 11th Army, facing westward, and the 12th Army, facing south towards the Terek Cossacks, who held the area around Petrovsk on the Caspian. At the start of January, General Denikin's forces attacked the 11th Army, breaking through the centre of their line, which had run from the lower reaches of the Caucasus Mountains north into the steppes.

On paper, the 11th Army had been a strong force, with around 150,000 troops, but they had been considerably weakened by disease and low morale. The supply line for the 11th Army back to the Soviet heartland was tenuous, stretching through Astrakhan and north along the Volga. At this stage, the Volunteer Army was mostly a genuine volunteer force, with high commitment and considerable experience. Spearheaded by General Wrangel's 1st Cavalry Division, the White forces could only field 25,000 fighting men. But this was enough to break the 11th Army, and Wrangel advanced along the rail line that runs south-east to the Caspian. Piatigorsk, which was the capital of the North Caucasus Soviet Republic, fell on 20 January. The Terek Cossacks attacked north and drove the Red 12th Army back towards Astrakhan. General Wrangel was given command of all the forces in the north Caucasus region.

On 1 January, SS *Riviera* entered the Black Sea carrying the first batch of men and aircraft of 221 Squadron. D. B. Knock described the trip across the Black Sea:

> 2/1/19 Worked the middle Watch, 12 to 4am, in bunkers shovelling coal. The war is over and all the duration men are growling. Better make the best of it and see what's coming.
> 3/1/19 Pulled into Batum harbour 10am. Snow capped Caucasus ranges frown over town in distance. Magnificent sight. Transport landed after ship tied up and CO [J. O. Andrews] orders me to get Ford ready for use. CO says will drive himself. Leaving jetty I go to jump out to open wide wooden gate onto road. CO snaps, 'Know my own judgement. I can easily get through there.' Takes it at 30mph and a rending crash sings the swan song of the port front mudguard. Difficult to restrain my inward mirth, but succeed. Out into town … Found military HQ. Whilst CO saw staff wallahs I got around handy and snagged a good meal from a cookhouse.[1]

Major Andrews' description of the arrival at Batum does not mention his accident with the Ford:

> The aircraft were quickly transferred to railway trucks at Batum whilst a visit to the (British) army HQ to obtain Intelligence and maps, proved fruitless. No maps were available. The squadron photographer made photographic copies of such maps as the army had, and the squadron proceeded leisurely across the Caucasus to Baku. The majority of the populace appeared averse to compulsory deliverance from the Red yoke, and consequently guards were mounted at each end of the train with rifles and Lewis guns. At every halt these detrained and took up positions, one each side of the train.[2]

Lieutenant Gayford was also on the train as it travelled across Transcaucasia:

> At Batum the aircraft were wheeled off the carrier and straight up on to flat railway trucks, their appropriate wings and empennage being lashed

alongside. All personnel were accommodated in Russian 3rd Class carriages, an excellent type of vehicle for long railway journeys. It had tree tiers of bunks, which can be folded down out of the way during the day. Our journey eastward across the Caucasus to Baku on the Caspian was a slow one, the line going West being congested with train loads of Turkish troops and repatriated prisoners returning to Turkey.[3]

The local population throughout the Caucasus was divided into numerous factions, including Georgian, Azerbaijani, and Armenian nationalists, supporters of the Soviet government and the White forces, plus many who just wanted to be left alone by everybody. Many of the groups making up the local population resented the arrival of the British forces in the area. The trip across the Caucasus was not without incident for Knock:

6/1/19 5pm train moves off. Steady gradient always climbing. When train stops, two must climb out and patrol the length of the train, one each side, with one in spout and fixed bayonet. 2am train stops and I am due for duty. Clamber out. Freezing cold and snow everywhere ... Wild looking surroundings. Creepy. Lofty Blake on other side of train.[4]

Knock was very nearly left behind when the train started off without warning. If he had been, he would have been lucky to survive the cold and the local inhabitants. As the journey continued, he turned once more to his diary:

Late afternoon passed through Tifflis, after brief halt. Wonderful Caucasian scenery, in which I revel.
7/1/19 Bowling through rolling plains and see two individuals with revolvers firing in direction of train. As it is my guard duty period, I let one round near them to scare them off. CO hears shots and enquires. Threatens me with close arrest, but as bullet holes were found through two Nine Ack [DH9A] fuselages hear nothing more about it. Those chaps must have been Bolsheviks.
9/1/19 Pass through country drab in colour and dotted with oil derricks. At 6pm we pull into Baku on the Caspian Sea.[5]

Although the British controlled the area around Baku, the numbers of British troops involved were never large enough to do more than have a presence in the major towns. The relations between the British and the various groups of locals, apart from the White forces the British had come to support, were never other than strained. Gayford recorded the following description of Baku:

Baku was indescribable confusion, and the whole political situation was changing almost daily, so having learned nothing we continued our journey to Petrovsk. Enroute we stopped at Derbent and were somewhat shaken to experience for the first time, what we were to get more accustomed to later, Cossack hospitality. They were astonished when we would not stay and continue the party indefinitely but said that we must go on at the scheduled time.[6]

The Terek Cossacks were based around the Terek River and were in the process of driving the Red 12th Army back towards Astrakhan. Petrovsk, the intended base for 221, was a small port on the Caspian, just north of the Caucasus Mountains. At the time the squadron arrived there in January, they were close to the front lines and were isolated in an area where many different groups still continued to fight. Knock described the journey to Petrovsk:

11/1/19 Train pulls out. Destination Petrovsk, a port about 250 miles North. Stop at a place called Derbent, where mayor and satellites hand out eatables. Good feed of roast goose.
12/1/19 Arrive Petrovsk. Unload equipment and billeted in old school at place three miles from town called Petrovsk Kavkaski. Fair ground for 'drome here.[7]

Lieutenant Gayford also recorded his first impressions of Petrovsk:

On arrival at Petrovsk we found an excellent site for an aerodrome on the outskirts of the town with a railway siding running right

Panorama of the airfield at Petrovsk, showing the fence that was built to provide shelter.

onto it ... We ran our train up onto the aerodrome site, and wheeled the aircraft off and erected them. The weather was bad, snowstorms and gales. Also there were no hangars. We built a screen facing South East to give the aircraft and mechanics working them some protection.[8]

By January, the northern part of the Caspian was frozen over and the wind blowing across the ice was freezing cold. Major Andrews was faced with a Herculean task to get the aircraft serviceable, to create the organisation for a fighting squadron, and to look after his men in severe conditions. In Baku, he had been issued with what he described as a chest filled with the local currency, and he put this to good use:

The squadron personnel, though not filled with enthusiasm, proved very adaptable and the unit was soon able to fend for itself. Petrol was obtained from the oil fields at Baku and was of excellent quality. Rations and fuel were purchased locally, the meat ration on the 'hoof' to be 'prepared by the squadron'.[9]

The aircraft 221 had brought to Russia were DH9s. These are powered by liquid-cooled engines. It proved to be almost impossible to start the engines in the prevailing conditions at Petrovsk:

The difficulties with the engines owing to the damp and cold were very great. The united efforts of the squadron for an hour or more were often necessary to get one engine started. Hot water poured into one end of the circulating system froze before it reached the other end.[10]

The airfield at Petrovsk. In the background are the Caucasus Mountains.

DH9 D2803, which crashed in January 1919 at Petrovsk.

Major Andrews had brought one Bentley-engined Sopwith Camel with him for his own use. The air-cooled Bentley engine gave no problems, either in starting or running.

 Over the coming months, the airfield at Petrovsk was improved with the construction of several hangars, using local and squadron labour. This improved conditions for the airmen and promoted the serviceability of the aircraft. The living conditions for the squadron were still grim, however, as Knock recorded:

> 18/1/19 No joke trying to keep warm. Big log stove going in quarters and all available clothing used with blankets on bed. Still cold ... Have to break ice in a tub outside to get wash and water in mornings. Envy officers with leather flying kits to keep warm! What a country! Plenty of insects in these quarters. Big fellows, like paddle steamers! Bite like Hades, but too cold to get out once they start, so endure.[11]

By the end of the month, in spite of the conditions, the first contingent of 221 Squadron was established at Petrovsk and the rest of the squadron aircraft and personnel were beginning to arrive.

One of the main tasks of the squadron was the support of the British Naval ships on the Caspian, but the Red naval ships were frozen in their port at Astrakhan and the Navy could not get at them. The DH9s did not have the range to bomb Astrakhan from Petrovsk. At the end of the month, Knock wrote in his diary:

> 28/1/19 Most machines assembled and in flying order. Am returned to duty as an armourer. Appears there is real work ahead. Capts. Grigson

Right: Lieutenant O. R. Gayford. Left: Captain J. W. B. Grigson. The DH9 in the background is 2803, one of the aircraft transported to Petrovsk.

and Gayford make crash landing in a nine and write it off. Neither hurt. Very glad. Both popular officers.[12]

This was aircraft number D2803. Lieutenant L. H. Kemp arrived with one of the later groups of officers for 221 Squadron. He described his arrival at Batum:

> We weren't allowed to come into the harbour. The senior naval officer ordered us to anchor 3 miles out but during the night a terrific storm broke out and our anchor chain broke and so we were adrift. We were adrift all night. What happened eventually I don't know. We eventually did get another anchor and in the meantime a lot of damage was done and we lost 2 aeroplanes. We lost several lorries and it was remarkable that we didn't lose any of the men because they were sleeping in those lorries. Eventually we did get into the harbour and we tied up there.[13]

Commodore Norris returned during January, after his accident, to command the Royal Navy contingent. He had asked for twelve Coastal Motor Boats to be sent by rail overland from the Black Sea and these also started to arrive in January. The CMBs were small, fast torpedo-carrying boats built by Thornycroft Ltd. They were forty feet long and weighed 4.35 tons; with a 250-horsepower petrol engine, they had a top speed of 33.5 knots. Although they were quite small, the Coastal Motor Boats

HMS *Alader Youssanoff*, with two of 266 Squadron's Short 184s on the foredeck.

carried one torpedo and twin machine-guns. The SS *Alader Youssanoff* was converted into a seaplane carrier for two Short 184 seaplanes when they arrived. In addition, the *Sergie* and *Edinburgh Castle* were converted to carry two CMBs each.

During the month, A Flight from 17 Squadron had also become established at Batum. The squadron was based at an old Turkish airfield outside the port. Six DH9s had been sent and the flight was in the process of rigging the aircraft and settling in.

NOTES

[1] Knock, D. B., 'An Armourer's Diary', *Popular Flying*, May 1938, page 90
[2] National Archives, Andrews, J. O., War Experiences
[3] National Archives, Gayford, O. R., War Experiences
[4] Knock, D. B., 'An Armourer's Diary', *Popular Flying*, May 1938, page 92
[5] Ibid., page 92
[6] National Archives, Gayford, O. R., War Experiences
[7] Knock, D. B., 'An Armourer's Diary', *Popular Flying*, May 1938, page 92
[8] National Archives, Gayford, O. R., War Experiences
[9] National Archives, Andrews, J. O., War Experiences
[10] Ibid.
[11] Knock, D. B., 'An Armourer's Diary', *Popular Flying*, May 1938, page 92
[12] Ibid., page 92
[13] Kemp, L. H., unpublished memoir

Detail of picture on p. 177.

CHAPTER SIX

FEBRUARY 1919

General Wrangel continued the White advance against the Red 11th Army during February. Grozni, the capital of Chechnia, was captured on 5 February. This allowed a join-up with the Terek Cossacks and provided a rail link between Ekaterinodar and Petrovsk, although the rail line running along the foothills of the Caucasus Mountains was never completely safe. Very few of the Red forces managed to retreat to Astrakhan or Tsaritsin. The Volunteer Army took over 50,000 prisoners; a complete Red Army Group had been destroyed. On 15 February, Krasnov, the leader of the Don Cossacks, was forced out of office because of his backing for the Germans and replaced as Ataman by General Bogaevsky. In 1947, Krasnov was hanged in Moscow as a Nazi collaborator.

During February, Lieutenant General Briggs replaced General Poole in command of the British Mission. The Armed Forces of South Russia had established their headquarters at Ekaterinodar under the control of General Denikin. Alongside this, the British established their HQ. General Briggs brought with him the first small amounts of British military aid. On 23 February, the officer who was to command the RAF in south Russia arrived in Novorossisk. This was Major, Acting Colonel, A. C. Maund. He had joined the Canadian infantry at the start of the First World War and transferred to the RFC in 1916. He had been in Russia at the time of the Revolution, as part of the mission to aid the Russians. While with this mission, he had taken part in the fighting on the Eastern Front against the Germans, flying in a BE2E. Later, he had been transferred to Archangel to command the air component of the British intervention in north Russia. It was because of his extensive experiences in Russia that Maund had been chosen to command the RAF in south Russia. He established the RAF HQ alongside the Army HQ at Ekaterinodar. There have been several derogatory descriptions made of Maund during his time in south Russia;

perhaps the best that could be said was that he was an efficient staff officer rather than a leader of men.

Ekaterinodar was a large provincial Russian town on the east bank of the Kuban River. There were docks along the river, which gave access to the Black Sea through the Sea of Azov. The town had been involved in the export of agricultural produce from the rich north Caucasus area. It was also the capital city and centre for the Kuban Cossacks.

The commander of 62 Wing, Lieutenant Colonel Bowhill, began his journey to Petrovsk to take command early in February. Bowhill was described by Lieutenant C. N. H. Bilney in the following terms:

> ...a shortish red faced man with bushy ginger eyebrows, outwardly a little brusque but with a heart of gold and a great gift of leadership'.[1]

Bilney was travelling with Bowhill as baggage officer to the headquarters staff, but his real job was to get the seaplane base at Petrovsk ready for 266 Squadron, who would be arriving later with the Short 184 seaplanes. The commander of 266 Squadron was to be Captain J. A. Sadler, as he recorded in his log-book on 1 February:

> Took command of 437 Flight (Russian draft changed to 266 Squadron – 62 Wing).[2]

The two flights in 266 Squadron were 437 and 438, both stationed on Mudros in the Mediterranean. Bowhill and the wing staff left Lemnos in the middle of February on board the *Princess Ena*, an old Channel Island ship.

The ship stopped in Constantinople and the RAF men had a short time ashore, where Bilney managed to buy some cartridges for his home-made shotgun. Following the same route as 221 Squadron, the ship arrived in Batum after a rough crossing of the Black Sea. Bilney was less than impressed by his first view of Batum:

> We eventually arrived at Batum which was a depressing sight, absolutely run down, completely. There were piles of manganese ore on the quays awaiting export, but nothing to export it in and everything was derelict.[3]

The party travelled across the Caucasus by train, along with four of the naval CMBs:

> On a cold afternoon we left Batum and started out on what turned out to be a six day journey ... It was very cold, and soon after leaving Batum

we picked up snow which remained with us for the rest of the journey, in depths of up to 4 ft ... A lot of the country [along the Caspian] was flat and uninteresting but where the hills came down to the sea we had to cross valleys and though many of them were beautiful we did not enjoy them much as valleys meant bridges and most of these had been burnt during the fighting. From a truck you have a view vertically downwards, and just looking at the charred ends of sleepers between you and the valley bottom was not very reassuring.[4]

While Bilney and Bowhill were travelling towards Petrovsk, 221 Squadron had started operations against the Red Army. The squadron diary states that four DH9s flew the first combat operation on 3 February. Bombs were dropped on the towns of Kalinovskaya and Kizlyar. Grozni was seen to contain at least 1,000 cavalry, and at Shedrinskaya an armoured train was bombed and machine-gunned from 2,000 ft. The train fired back and the DH9 was hit. On 5 February, Grozni was again bombed:

Grozni attacked by one DH9. Barracks attacked with eight 16lb. bombs and 144 baby incendiary. Fire caused and many hits observed on buildings. Troops of horsemen with Red Flag attacked and dispersed with machine gun fire N.E. of town. Many casualties observed. Rolling stock for ten trains at station.[5]

During the day, Naurskaya was also bombed, and on the rail line a train was bombed by a DH9. A direct hit was obtained with two 65 lb bombs, destroying four trucks and partially derailing the train.

On 5 February, the advancing White forces captured Grozni. The cavalry that was attacked north-east of Grozni may have been White cavalry. Noting this incident in his diary, Knock wrote:

Two Nine Acks [DH9As] go on reconnaissance North each with two 65 and one 230 pound bombs. South of Astrakhan they spot a parade of cavalry, with red pennons flying. Drop the pills and get photos. Return and develop in glee showing much carnage. One up against the Reds.

13/2/19 Cossack officer of high rank arrives with interpreter. Story gets round. That was no Red cavalry bombed, but the side we are supposed to be assisting. Our 'planes decimated a squadron of White cavalry. WT man tells me that SNO [Senior Naval Officer] Caspian has ordered 221 to cease activity until further orders. Thought that Cossack looked furious. No wonder.[6]

There is no mention of this incident in the squadron records or the squadron diary. If it did actually occur, Knock does not seem to have been too bothered.

The rank and file of the RAF force had not volunteered for duty in Russia and now that the 'real' war against Germany was over, most of them just wanted to get home. They had no real understanding of the issues involved, or even the forces involved, or what they were doing stationed at a port on the Caspian Sea. Some of them were not even sure what side they were on. Knock had earlier written:

> 5/2/19 Realise that we are actually attached to Denikin's White Army here.[7]

It is always a good idea in war to know whose side you are on.

On 8 February, Major Andrews flew a reconnaissance in his personal Camel, looking for advanced landing strips, but none were found. Describing the first week's operations, the squadron diary states:

> The weather for the week has been bad, high winds, mist and low clouds. The attacks on the 5th made on trains, barracks, etc. were very successful and were carried out from low altitudes with skill and daring, in spite of heavy barrage of rifle and machine gun fire. The machines were hit frequently and two were forced to descend about 50 miles away from their aerodrome, owing to damage due to enemy fire. One crashed badly on landing, the other was burnt by the pilot to prevent it falling into enemy hands. Pilots and observers managed to return safely to the aerodrome.[8]

The loss of two aircraft out of the three involved shows the extent of the ground fire the DH9s had faced.

During the rest of the month, the weather continued to be bad, only allowing the occasional operation. On 9 February, a reconnaissance was carried out along the rail line that runs north-west towards Ekaterinodar and had just been captured from the Reds. The DH9 carried a British engineering officer as a passenger. Another reconnaissance was carried out north along the coast on 15 February. Three DH9s bombed a Red ship trapped in the ice on 18 February. Only one direct hit was obtained. The crew escaped across the ice and were machine-gunned by one of the DH9s.

The DH9s did not have the range to bomb Astrakhan from Petrovsk. On 22 February, a DH9 reconnoitred Chechen Island, looking for an advance landing ground to shorten the distance to Astrakhan, but nothing

A DH9A landing at Petrovsk airfield. Note the Caucasus Mountains in the background, the highest mountains in Europe.

was seen owing to the bad weather. For the rest of the month, only a few practice flights were carried out. The squadron diary states:

> Owing to the advance of the Volunteer Army and the fact that there is no Liaison Officer now with them, no bombing for this Army could be carried out as their movements are uncertain.[9]

The Volunteer Army had joined forces with the Terek Cossacks and was driving the Red Army back towards Astrakhan.

The conditions in Petrovsk were extremely unsettled. British troops were told only to go out in pairs and to avoid certain parts of the town. Lieutenant L. H. Kemp, with the RAF contingent, wrote about the situation:

> We had a lot of incidents really. We were billeted in a school and the odd bullet would fly past the window at night.[10]

A number of Army personnel were killed in Petrovsk during the British time there and their killers were never found.

D. B. Knock seems to have settled in better than some of the officers:

> 15/2/19 Make a friend in one Waldemar Zagorsky Russian non-com, pilot attached to us. Shows me the ropes in Petrovsk Port and we

have much fun together. He speaks French. I teach him English and he responds with Russian. Getting things off fine now. Can hold almost a normal conversation in Russian. Waldy can hold his vodka and shows me how! Introduces me to Zenia, sister of lady friend.[11]

With the Bolshevik fleet frozen in at Astrakhan, there was no contact between the Red navy and the British ships on the Caspian. But the British ships did continue to patrol the line of the ice in case any ships did break out, as the Reds were equipped with ice-breakers.

NOTES

[1] Bilney, C. N. H., unpublished memoir
[2] Sadler, J. A., log-book
[3] Bilney, C. N. H., unpublished memoir
[4] Ibid.
[5] National Archives , 62 Wing diary
[6] Knock D. B., 'An Armourer's Diary', *Popular Flying*, May 1938, page 92
[7] Ibid., page 92
[8] National Archives, 62 Wing diary
[9] Ibid.
[10] Kemp, L. H., unpublished memoir
[11] Knock, D. B., 'An Armourer's Diary', *Popular Flying*, May 1938, page 146

CHAPTER SEVEN

MARCH 1919

During March, the Don Cossack Army was able to regain some of the territory it had lost. The Cossacks advanced to the north but were never able to capture Tsaritsin to the east. General Wrangel was severely ill with typhus during the month of March, and most of his troops were transferred to the left wing of the Volunteer Army in the Donitz area. Only the cavalry division under the command of General Ulagai was left in the north Caucasus area, and this was not strong enough to continue the advance towards Astrakhan. The first British ship carrying military supplies for General Denikin arrived in Novorossisk during March.

Captain Sadler, the commanding officer of 266 Squadron, had left Mudros on 18 February on board HMS *Engadine* with the first group of men and aircraft for the squadron. By 1 March, they were in Batum waiting to be transported to Petrovsk port. Also on the same day, Lieutenant Bilney arrived in Petrovsk to set up the base for 266:

> ...arrived at Petrovsk on March 1st. This was a small town of 4/5000 inhabitants and owed its existence to its good but quite small harbour. The town was under deep snow when we arrived and we didn't get rid of it for some time. The British force consisted of a Company of Punjabis, relieved at a later date by Ghurkhas. The town Major had arranged quarters for us in the Anglo Asiatic Bank building, and this remained Wing HQ throughout our stay.[1]

Using local labour, Bilney organised the conversion of a wool warehouse at the side of the harbour into living quarters for the squadron airmen. Open-sided sheds were used as hangars for the aircraft and other storage sheds were converted into workshops.

Short 184 being lifted into the water at Petrovsk port. Captain Sadler was right in observing that the crane was too small.

A mobile crane to lift the seaplanes onto the water was found and installed alongside the quay. Counting Captain Sadler, eight officers and fifty-one ratings arrived with six aircraft in Petrovsk on 10 March. The officers went into billets at the meteorological office. When the machines were unpacked from their crates, it was found that the vital exhaust manifolds were missing and these had to be constructed locally by the squadron mechanics. The second half of the squadron arrived on 20 March with four more aircraft.

The chronic bad weather was still limiting flying by 221 Squadron. On 13 March, several demonstration flights were made over the local countryside to impress the locals. A DH9 crashed into the sea during one of these flights, which cannot have impressed the locals too much. The pilot and observer were rescued. This was the fourth aircraft lost. The squadron records state that 'the daily sick attendance at 221 Squadron is high'. Extreme weather, bad conditions, and poor morale were starting to affect the squadron. Even the redoubtable D. B. Knock was affected:

17/3/19 Develop chronic teeth trouble, followed by fever of some kind. High temperature. MO cannot diagnose. Says I must be sent to Baku hospital.
18/3/19 Loaded on train for Baku along with two other chaps, and after rotten trip arrive there on 19th. On my back for days. Fever dies slowly

and teeth bad. Convalescent and report to military dentist on 30th. Five teeth to fix up.[2]

Most of the officers and men had spent the First World War in the eastern Mediterranean and the cold in Russia must have come as a shock.

On 24 March, a demonstration flight was made over Petrovsk. Three DH9s also made a demonstration flight over Baku on 25 March. On the same day, a flight was made to Chechen Island to find a suitable landing field for an advanced base. It was found that the island was still iced up, but a likely landing ground was found for the future. Other demonstration flights were made on 27, 28, 30, and 31 March. But no effective liaison had been established with the White Armies, and the British aircrew did not know which were Red Army and which were Volunteer Army units, thus enabling them to carry out effective attacks.

Commodore Norris finally managed to disband the Centro-Caspian Flotilla during March after the CMBs fired two torpedoes at ships of the Flotilla. The sailors of the Flotilla decided that discretion was the better part of valour and abandoned their vessels. While the Bolshevik fleet was iced in at Astrakhan, the British ships were now the only effective naval force on the Caspian. Three of the Flotilla's ships were taken over by the British and renamed the *Windsor Castle*, *Dublin Castle*, and *Orlionoch*,

Five Coastal Motor Boats alongside HMS *Kruger* in Baku harbour on 1 March 1919 during the surrender of the Centro-Caspian Flotilla.

which later replaced the *Alader Youssanoff* as the seaplane carrier. Four of the CMBs were stationed at Baku, four at Petrovsk, and four were carried on the two ships. As more ships were taken over, some of the older ships were paid off. The number of ships available to the British never exceeded eight armed merchantmen, two CMB carriers, and one seaplane carrier.

By the end of March, both 221 and 266 were in place at Petrovsk, waiting for the extreme winter weather to break so they could play a part in the war against the Red forces.

NOTES

[1] Bilney, C. N. H., unpublished memoir
[2] Knock, D. B., 'An Armourer's Diary', *Popular Flying*, May 1938, page 146

CHAPTER EIGHT

APRIL 1919

At the start of April, General Wrangel was still too ill to take part in the fighting. The Don Cossack army was under pressure in the north, and the Volunteer Army was being forced back in the area north of the Crimea and the Donitz area. Stationed at Tsaritsin was the Soviet 10th Red Army, reinforced with the remnants of the 11th Army. During April, this force began a major advance south-west along the rail line running between Tsaritsin and Ekaterinodar. In command was General Egorov; the leader of his cavalry forces was General Dumenko. The weakened White forces were driven back, and Dumenko's cavalry advanced to within fifty miles of Rostov. If this advance had been allowed to continue, the Armed Forces of South Russia would have been cut in two.

As the result of a disagreement with General Denikin, Wrangel refused to take command of the White forces to block the advance. This forced Denikin to take personal command, the last time he commanded forces in the field. Denikin managed to stabilise the situation on the west bank of the Manych River. In his memoirs, Wrangel claimed that Denikin begged him to take command of the counter-attack, and he finally agreed to do so at the end of the month.

Conditions for the men at 221 Squadron were still grim. During the month, Major Andrews was invalided home:

> In April I contracted typhus whilst on a ground reconnaissance north of Petrovsk. The Squadron Medical Officer had no experience with this fever, and the medical supplies were inadequate, but the deficiencies were made good by the despatch from Baku of a Welsh miner, turned Nursing Orderly, who had been through the Serbian retreat. In future I would not light-heartedly set out on an expedition, in a pestilence-stricken country, without a knowledgeable medical staff and suitable medical stores.[1]

The armourer Knock, meanwhile, was still receiving medical treatment in Baku.

The plan to create the advanced base on Chechen Island, seventy miles north of Petrovsk, was put into practice. Chechen Island was described as an uninhabited sand bank, and the nearest mainland was just within range of Red Army cavalry patrols. The island was not a popular base among the RAF men. The Royal Navy also used the island as an anchorage for their ships. Early in the month, demonstration flights were carried out when the weather permitted. Colonel Bowhill wrote in the Wing diary:

> Demonstration flights are carried out fairly frequently as some of the small towns and villages close to this place are reported to be openly Bolshevik. I am standing by to bomb these if ordered. The advanced party for Chechen Island has proceeded.[2]

On 6 April, four DH9s set out for Chechen to refuel and go on to bomb Astrakhan, but they were forced to return because of fog. The same thing happened on 7 and 8 April as bad weather continued to frustrate the planned attacks on Astrakhan. Demonstration flights continued when possible. On 12 April, one machine left Petrovsk for Grozni with despatches from General Pryevalsky to General Denikin.

DH9s on the ground at Petrovsk.

Early in the month, the *Ark Royal* arrived in Batum with the first six DH9A aircraft for the squadron. The machines were transported by rail to Petrovsk. The DH9A was a slightly larger machine than the DH9 and had a large, more reliable engine. This allowed the aircraft a longer range and greater bomb load.

A demonstration flight over the village of Koumtor Kale on 13 April was fired on, and the DH9 returned fire. Attempts to bomb Astrakhan were again frustrated by bad weather. On 14 April, four DH9s left Petrovsk and landed at Chechen. After taking off once again, however, they were forced by fog to turn back to Chechen and became stranded there. The bad weather severely hampered operations, as recorded in the Wing diary for 19 April:

> Machines attempted to reach Astrakhan but were forced to return owing to fog. At noon in response to a signal that HMS *Asia* was engaging two hostile destroyers, machines left Chechen to attack same. Destroyers, who had broken off engagement, were not discovered owing to thick mist, in spite of the fact that machines returned to Chechen, filled up and went in search a second time.[3]

Now that the ice had melted, Bolshevik ships had started to move south into the Caspian from Astrakhan.

HMS *Asia*.

The bombing of Astrakhan was finally achieved on 21 April. A major delta is formed where the River Volga runs into the Caspian Sea; Astrakhan is situated on one of the many channels making up the estuary. The DH9s carried out a reconnaissance of the main channel and bombed some of the ships that they found there. A large amount of shipping was reported in this main channel. A gunboat was attacked at Harbay, and another north of Harbay.

The main Bolshevik fleet was reported at anchor in a side channel at Mogilny. Two motor launches in the main channel were machine-gunned and the main rail line was bombed. In all, the aircraft reported seeing five armed merchant ships, seven destroyers, six gunboats, two depot ships, and ten motor launches. The longest flight was four hours and forty minutes, covering 360 miles, including 270 over the sea – no mean feat with the notoriously unreliable DH9s.

The bad weather returned for the rest of the month, preventing any further attack on Astrakhan. A few demonstration flights were undertaken; one in the area of Grozni reported large numbers of cavalry and that the oil wells north and south of the town were burning, fired by the local Chechens. The squadron diary notes that fighting between the Volunteer Army and the Chechens started on 21 April. A British company owned the oil wells around Grozni, and the manager complained that the fires were costing three million roubles a day.

The entry in the Wing diary of 221 Squadron for 27 April notes that:

> Machine when dropping rations to pilot and observer of machine which had a forced landing at Kosa Utsch, had a forced landing and crashed pilot and observer returned on foot 50 miles.[4]

These would seem to have been the fifth and sixth DH9s lost by the squadron.

Now that the ice had melted and freed the Red ships, more of 221 Squadron's time would be spent supporting the Royal Navy ships on the Caspian:

> On receipt of signal from Commodore Caspian that enemy ships were out, machine left Chechen and attacked two enemy ships 75 miles north of Chechen the ships immediately altered course 16 points and returned to their base. Bombs dropped within 20 feet of ships and may have damaged them. Machine subjected to AA fire from ships.[5]

Although they had not been hit, the ships had been turned back.

At this time, the Red air force had a number of units in Astrakhan. Two of these units were equipped with flying boats (M5 and M9 types);

there were also small numbers of Russian-built SPADs, Nieuports, and Sopwith 1½ Strutters. All these aircraft had been well used and were in poor condition. Most of the Imperial air force pilots had joined the White forces, and most of the Red pilots lacked experience. There was also a severe shortage of aviation petrol. This shortage of decent aircraft and petrol meant that the newer pilots never obtained the necessary flying hours to gain expertise.

266 Squadron had brought with them ten brand-new Maori III-engined Short 184 seaplanes. By 3 April, the first of them had been rigged and the new exhaust manifold manufactured. Captain Sadler took the first aircraft for a forty-minute flight. He wrote in his log-book:

> Locally around Petrovsk Caspian. Test Flight of newly erected aircraft, tail heavy, good. Engine with new standard manifolds twin exhaust pipes. Rather difficult getting aircraft onto water owing to smallness of crane.[6]

As an inland sea, the Caspian is considerably less saline than real sea water, and the northern part of the sea, where most of the rivers run into it, is even less salty. This meant that the floats on the Short 184 sank deeper into the water than normal, forcing them to need considerably longer take-off runs. The remedy was an airscrew with a finer pitch, allowing the Short higher acceleration at lower speeds. The nearest place that produced propellers was Malta, and an urgent signal was made for the correct propellers to be sent.

Short 184 on the dock at Petrovsk port.

Short 184 N9081, which crashed on its first flight on 25 April 1919 with Captain
Sadler at the controls. It was later repaired and operated from one of the seaplane
carriers.

On 25 April, Captain Sadler was carrying out the first test flight of
Short 184 number 9081: as he tried to lift the aircraft off the water a
sudden gust of wind turned the aircraft, causing damage to both starboard
wings. The aircraft was towed back by a naval launch and hoisted out
of the water onto the jetty for repairs. On 26 April, 266 Squadron flew a
first operation, with one aircraft flying from Petrovsk to Chechen Island,
refuelling, and then carrying out a reconnaissance to the north before
returning to Petrovsk.

On 30 April, the seaplane carrier HMS *Alader Youssanoff* entered
the harbour at Petrovsk to embark the aircraft. As part of the scheme to
support General Denikin's forces, it had been decided to base one RAF
squadron with the main part of Denikin's Army. 47 Squadron had been
based in Salonika during the First World War, and it was this squadron
that was used as the basis for the squadron sent to south Russia. Half
of 47 Squadron and half of 17 Squadron, also based in Salonika, were
chosen to go. On 16 April, eleven officers and the necessary mechanics
and armourers for one flight left for Novorossisk. Later in the month, ten
officers from 17 Squadron were transferred to south Russia, including
Captain S. G. Frogley, who had been stationed in Batum with A Flight.
Captain Frogley was to command the squadron in Russia. None of this
first batch of officers and men had volunteered to go to Russia.

South Russia, showing the main rail lines and the area of operations for 47
Squadron.

Whippet tanks on the way to the front line.

The SS *Warpointer* arrived in Novorossisk on 24 April carrying the first load of stores, transport, and machines for the RAF. The aircraft were not new but had been transferred from Salonika. An airfield close to the racecourse in Ekaterinodar was to be the squadron base while they rigged the DH9s and established exactly what the Russians wanted from them.

The British Military Mission HQ in Ekaterinodar also established a tank training school in the town. The first commander of the tank school was Major N. McMickling, who arrived in Russia from France with ten officers and fifty-five other ranks on 13 April 1919. With this first detachment were six Mark V heavy tanks and six Medium A Whippet tanks. Again, most of the British other ranks were not volunteers and were resentful at being sent to Russia when the 'real war', as they saw it, was over.

An experienced tank officer, Major E. M. Bruce, was given overall command of the British tank forces in south Russia in late April. Major Bruce had lost an arm during the fighting on the Western Front in France. The first Russian tank crews were given only a minimal amount of training, as the tanks were desperately needed at the front line.

By the end of April, the ice in the northern part of the Caspian had cleared and the Red ships began to leave their sanctuary in the north. As noted earlier, on 19 April the *Asia* had a long-range artillery duel with two Bolshevik ships, which were able to escape, using their greater speed. Later in the month, the Red ships were sighted at sea in the northern part of the Caspian and several minor actions took place, with no losses on either side.

By the end of April, British assistance to the armed forces of south Russia was beginning to move into position.

NOTES

[1] National Archives , Andrews, J. O., War Experiences
[2] National Archives, 62 Wing diary
[3] Ibid.
[4] Ibid.
[5] Ibid.
[6] Sadler, J. A., log-book

Detail of picture on p. 190.

CHAPTER NINE

MAY 1919

At the beginning of May, General Wrangel was still commanding the forces holding the Red 10th Army on the Manych River, a tributary of the River Don. The Manych River runs south to north at right angles to the main Ekaterinodar to Tsaritsin rail line. Most of the forces under Wrangel's command were Kuban and Terek Cossacks, and this group of forces was renamed the Caucasus Army.

The disposition of the Armed Forces of South Russia at this time was as follows. On the western flank facing the Donitz area, north of the Crimea, were the original remnants of the Volunteer Army under General Mai-Maevsky, a brilliant but erratic general. The Don Cossack forces, meanwhile, were attempting to regain the northern parts of their territory under their new commander, General Sidorin. General Wrangel himself was facing the Red forces attempting to break through to Rostov. In the south-east, General Erdel was commanding the Dagestan Army trying to take Astrakhan.

The area around Velikoknyajeskaya, on the Manych River, was marshy and difficult for heavy transport. After failing to cross the river at several fords because of the heavily dug-in Red troops on the opposite bank, Wrangel was forced to wait for reinforcements. General Dumenko, the Red cavalry leader, tried to outflank the River Manych by moving eighty miles to the south, but Wrangel's own cavalry leader, General Ulagai, blocked this and the Red Army suffered heavy casualties. On 19 May, General Wrangel forced a crossing of the Manych eight miles south of Velikoknyajeskaya, using hundreds of picket fences taken from local houses. After three days of fighting, the 10th Army was forced back along the rail line towards Tsaritsin, 200 miles away, leaving 15,000 prisoners.

The White air force had played a major part in Wrangel's victory. Two White air force units, comprising ten aircraft, had carried out a series of

attacks on 20 May and had broken up the cavalry counter-attack launched
by the Red Army. Colonel Maund described the incident:

> During successful Volunteer Army attack on Tsaritsin railway at Manych
> River crossing May 29th [Maund got the date wrong] Russian air force,
> by successful bombing and machine gun attack on massed Bolshevik
> cavalry, when latter was preparing to attack main Volunteer Army force
> that had succeeded in crossing river Manych, completely disorganised
> Bolsheviks and panicked horses. They were then routed and with the
> assistance of aeroplanes were driven off the field. This was the critical
> stage battle and led to the capture of the entire 37th Bolshevik infantry
> division following day.[1]

The commander of the 1st Kuban Air Detachment, Colonel V. M.
Tkatcheff, was shot in the foot by ground fire during low level attacks.
Attached to the 10th Army, the Red air force had fourteen aircraft, but
these had been only averaging three sorties a month each and made no
effort to stop the White air force over the Manych River.

The weather over the Caspian Sea continued to be poor, restricting the
number of raids on Astrakhan that could be carried out by 221 Squadron.
On 4 May, information was received that Petrovsk was to be attacked by
up to 3,000 insurgent troops, and all the British forces were put on stand-
by, including the RAF forces. But when, later in the day, a reconnaissance
was carried out, nothing was found of the attacking force. Armourer D. B.
Knock had recovered from his illness and reported back to Petrovsk on 3
May in the midst of this emergency:

> 3/5/19 At Petrovsk. Report to squadron. Back on armoury duties. Find
> that Major Andrews had contracted typhus, partially recovered, and left
> for England. His place taken by Major De Ville, whom I saw fly into
> Horsea WT tower in 1917.
> 4/5/19 Sudden alarm in small hours. Doors and windows barricaded and
> Lewises ready. Reported Bolshevik advance in vicinity. All officers and
> men prepare to defend the place. Let a few tracers from Lewises out into
> the night. Nothing happens.[2]

Captain Sadler also noted in his log-book that 266 Squadron personnel
were awakened at 04.30 hours and had to go to 'action stations'.

The troubles around Petrovsk continued and an Army sergeant was
killed by a grenade on 5 May. On 7 May, the weather was acceptable and
four aircraft took off from Chechen Island for a reconnaissance of the area
north of the island, where it had been reported that Red forces had landed

The officers of 266 Squadron.

from the sea. Nothing was seen, but a paddle steamer that appeared to
be aground was bombed. One DH9 made a forced landing on the way
back, but the crew managed to restart the engine and return to Chechen.
Another attack was mounted on Astrakhan on 10 May. Four aircraft took
off from Chechen to bomb shipping in the main channel into Astrakhan.
One machine was forced to return with engine difficulties. The other three
observed a considerable amount of shipping:

> At Mogilny the seaplane station and Volga barges were bombed. The
> seaplane station was hit with 100lb bomb, which deleted 3 or 4 F.B.A.
> Flying Boats, standing outside hangar. At Harbay and vicinity stores
> sheds and Volga barges were bombed, hits being obtained on both. Fires
> were started in the stores. Machines were fired on by A.A. guns from
> barges, but these were silenced by machine gun fire from machines.[3]

The four-hour flights required by the bombing attacks on Astrakhan
must have been an unnerving experience for the aircrew in the unreliable
DH9s.

In general, the weather for most of the month was unsuitable for long-
range flying. The weather had now warmed up, but it was high wind and fog
that limited flights. Nonetheless, on 14 May the first raid by a single DH9A
from Petrovsk took place. The main Bolshevik fleet had left the Astrakhan
area, but an armed tug towing a barge was bombed and driven ashore. An
armed trawler was also bombed and machine-gunned from 700 ft.

Four DH9s left Petrovsk on 15 May for Chechen Island. One of the aircraft crashed on landing and burned out. The pilot, Lieutenant B. E. Nelson-Turner, and the observer, Second Lieutenant G. E. Jemmeson, were both killed. D. B. Knock wrote about the crash in his diary:

16/5/19 Tragic day. Lieutenant Nelson-Turner and Obs. Lieutenant Jemmeson crash in a DH9 landing at Chechen. Went up in flames and had no hope. Rotten to think that Nelson-Taylor finished like that. He was frank to me at times that he hadn't the nerve he possessed when passing out at flying school at home. Am told that they must have been killed by the impact before the fire as it was a very bad smash-up.[4]

It seems unlikely that an officer would have confided in an other rank in this way, but morale did seem to be declining generally the longer the squadron was in Russia:

10/5/19 Mass meeting of O.Rs. and soap box oratory by two who take a vote on a decision 'that the C. O. shall immediately through the Wing Commander communicate with the Air Ministry to ask what steps are being taken for relief of squadron'. Would be glad to get home myself.[5]

Most of the servicemen who had volunteered or been conscripted for the First World War had now been demobbed, and the forces in south Russia, men who had not seen their families for years, were not pleased with the thought that all the postwar jobs would have been filled by the time they finally arrived home.

In his diary, Knock added:

29/5/19 Commodore commanding Caspian naval forces [Commodore Norris] addresses parade and appeals to us to carry on in the interests of humanity and peace of the world.
30/5/19 Mosquitoes taking toll. Chronic fevers attacking many fellows. My legs and arms a mass of bites. But lucky so far ... We are asked to volunteer for service with General Denikin as instructors in the Russian Volunteer Aviation Service. No response. Everybody getting fed up.[6]

At a later date, a number of the officers did volunteer to continue to serve in south Russia.

The Red ships that had left Astrakhan were finally located at Fort Alexandrovsk, on the eastern shore of the Caspian. A raid was mounted on this fleet by DH9As from Petrovsk on 18 May. A large number of ships were found, but no direct hits were observed. One of the aircraft was hit by machine-gun fire, but returned safely. As more DH9As were becoming available, the DH9s were being handed over to the White Russian air force. Several reconnaissance flights were carried out from Chechen Island along the coast north of the island. Ships that had been landing Red troops behind the front line were bombed. Lieutenant Leavsley crashed one of the DH9s (number D2797) on 20 May, the seventh DH9 lost.

A major naval engagement took place in Alexandrovsk on 21 May, as described later. No ships were found in Fort Alexandrovsk when a reconnaissance was carried out on 26 May and a bombing raid of the Astrakhan area by five DH9s from Chechen Island on 27 May revealed the fact that most of the fleet had returned to Astrakhan. Shipping in the main channel was bombed, as were buildings at Harbay. Lieutenant John Brayne Lynch, one of the pilots in 221 Squadron, wrote in his log-book:

> 27/5/19 08.20hrs. DH9 2958, Observer Lt. Gould, Time in Air 3hrs. 30mins. Height 5,000 ft. Carrying 8 16lb and 2 100lb bombs. Lt. Borth returned with engine trouble. Sighted Bolshevik fleet off Delta. (Comprising TBDs MLs and tugs.) 30 strong. Bombed and machine gunned them. 1 submarine sighted 5 miles S W of force.[7]

Demonstration flights continued over the surrounding villages and leaflets were dropped. Four aircraft trying to reach Astrakhan were turned back by bad weather on 30 May. The DH9As carried out another raid on Astrakhan on 31 May. Shipping, tugs, and barges were bombed. The main fleet was not seen, leading to the conclusion that it must have gone farther up the Volga. Several of the aircraft were hit by AA fire. Bombing raids to Astrakhan from Petrovsk, incidentally, involved a flight of 520 miles, mostly over water.

It was also during May that 266 Squadron began to join 221 Squadron in combat sorties around the Caspian. On 1 May, Lieutenant Bilney was posted to command A Flight of 266 Squadron, with the acting rank of Captain. The Wing diary for 1 May reads:

> Seaplane while on patrol from Chechen to 12 foot anchorage, sighted in S. I. a steam tug towing three large barges proceeding W. S. W., barges apparently carrying troops. These were bombed, bombs falling within 20 feet of barges. Fire with machine gun was opened on barges. Numerous local flights carried out.[8]

Other reconnaissance flights were flown on 4, 6, and 8 May, but nothing was seen. A major ammunition convoy for the Ural Cossacks was escorted from Petrovsk to Guryev on 7 May, but again no Red ships were sighted.

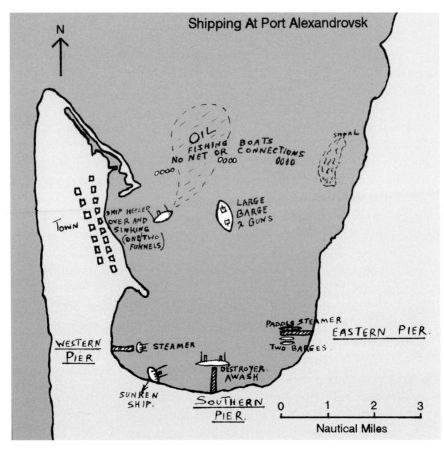

Sketch map showing the situation in Fort Alexandrovsk harbour after the last raid by Short 184s on 22 May 1919. Based on a map drawn by a 184 observer.

221 Squadron aircraft dropping bombs on shipping at Harbay on the River Volga, close to Astrakhan.

A sunken Bolshevik destroyer photographed after the attack on 21 May 1919 at Fort Alexandrovsk.

On the morning of 12 May, the seaplane carrier *Alader Youssanoff*, equipped with two Short 184 seaplanes (numbers N9080 and N9082), left Petrovsk.. The Short 184s were large, ungainly aircraft used to carry out low-level machine-gun attacks and support British shipping. Captain Bilney left the following description of the *Alader Youssanoff*:

> This ship was a merchantman, and by clearing the fore deck and rigging a derrick to the foremast we were able to stow two seaplanes side by side with their wings folded. On the poop deck we had a 4" gun, but as it was No.1 Mk1 of its particular series and built in 1898 I am very glad we never had to fire it. Our skipper was a grand chap, Lt. Chiltern, R.N.R., and we carried two seamen as quartermasters and two Royal Marines to keep order! The rest of the ship's officers and crew were Russians, and proved to be most unreliable.[9]

A major operation was planned by the British ships on the Caspian to carry out a reconnaissance of the Alexandrovsk area. If the Bolshevik fleet was in the harbour at Alexandrovsk, the seaplanes and the CMBs would attack it. As the British squadron of three armed ships and three carriers closed on Alexandrovsk on 15 May, four Bolshevik armed ships towing two barges were seen. The armed ships cast off the barges and escaped into

Alexandrovsk. Having been abandoned, the two barges displayed white flags and surrendered. When the barges were boarded, they were found to contain firewood and coal. Commander Norris described the white flag on one of the barges:

> When we hauled down the flag of truce, we found that it was not a flag at all, but a pair of unmentionable undergarments belonging to an old lady of sixty, who was one of the crew of the barge. It was proposed to send it to the War Museum. But this was not done.[10]

After the crews were taken off, both barges were sunk. The prisoners confirmed that most of the Bolshevik fleet was now in Alexandrovsk.

Heavy winds blew on 16 and 17 May, forcing the British ships to move south. Late on 17 May, the two seaplanes carried by the *Alader Youssanoff* were hoisted out onto the water to attempt a bombing raid on Alexandrovsk, but due to the high winds both aircraft were damaged. Lieutenant H. G. Pratt, the observer on one of the seaplanes, wrote the following in his log-book:

> 17/5/19 Wind Direction and Velocity NW, Machine Type Short 9082, Pilot Lieutenant R. G. K. Morrison, To bomb Alexandrovitch [sic], Flight from seaplane carrier Alader Youssanoff. Sea much too rough had to drop all bombs. No good. Elevator, float and wing smashed coming in.[11]

The seaplane carrier steamed back to Petrovsk to obtain more aircraft, escorted by the *Emile Nobel*. With only two armed ships left, Commodore Norris carried out a patrol north towards Astrakhan and then back towards Petrovsk.

The *Alader Youssanoff* and three more ships rendezvoused with Commodore Norris on 19 May. His squadron now included the armed ships *Kruger*, *Windsor Castle*, *Emile Nobel*, *Ventuir*, and *Asia*, along with the seaplane carrier and two CMB carriers. By the morning of 20 May, the squadron was in position fifty miles south of Alexandrovsk. The two Short seaplanes were hoisted out and launched. One of the aircraft crashed on take-off, but the other one carried out a successful bombing attack on the ships in the harbour at Alexandrovsk. The aircraft that crashed was 9077, piloted by Morrison with Pratt as his observer. The Short was a complete write-off, and the crew clung to the wreckage until they were picked up. Leaving the three lightly armed carriers to the south, Norris steamed north and positioned his ships outside the harbour at Alexandrovsk.

The weather on 21 May proved to be fine, and shortly after midnight the British ships closed in on the harbour. At daybreak, a considerable

HMS *Emile Nobel.*

The wreckage of Short 184 N9079, with Lieutenant R. G. K. Morrison and
Lieutenant H. G. Pratt clinging to the floats. The aircraft crashed on take-off on 20
May 1919 while attempting to carry out a reconnaissance of Fort Alexandrovsk.

Bombs exploding close to the armed ice-breaker *Caspi* in Fort Alexandrovsk
harbour, photographed on 22 May 1919 from an attacking Short 184.

number of craft could be seen moving about within the port. Two more British armed ships were steaming north to join the squadron, but Norris decided the moment had come to press home his attack. The harbour at Fort Alexandrovsk is V-shaped, with the V running north and south and around six miles long. On the eastern side are high cliffs and headlands; to the west the shore is shallow with a series of sandbanks. All navigation marks had been removed.

As the British ships steamed across the mouth of the harbour, several Russian craft outside the harbour opened fire. A number of ships were cut off from the port and steamed north, playing no further part in the engagement. A large barge at the entrance to the harbour, armed with six-inch guns, was hit and put out of action. The Caspian armed ice-breaker was also hit. As they reached the mouth of the harbour, the British ships turned south into the port, steaming in line ahead.

The Russian ships opened fire but also tried to retreat farther south into the port. Only one of the British ships could fire directly ahead, so the ships turned to starboard and positioned themselves across the harbour. Artillery pieces on the shore, as well as the guns on the Russian ships, were now firing at the British vessels. The *Emile Nobel* was hit in the engine room and several men were killed. Lieutenant Gardener, in the engine room, managed to repair the damage done to the engines and the *Emile Nobel* was able to keep steam up. Large clouds of smoke were seen to be coming from the direction of the Bolshevik ships, and the British ships were reduced to firing on the gun flashes in the smoke. One enemy shell hit the *Kruger*, the British flagship, but damage was minimal.

Firing had started at 12.13 hours, and by 13.30 hours Commodore Norris decided that, as most of the Bolshevik ships had been hit, it would be better to pull out of the harbour before any more of the British ships were damaged. It was planned to call up the three carriers and carry out a torpedo attack the next day with the CMBs. After the five British ships had steamed out of sight of Alexandrovsk, the *Emile Nobel* was forced to stop to carry out repairs to the engines. Large explosions and clouds of smoke could be seen coming from the direction of Alexandrovsk. An attempt was made to contact the three carriers that were still south of Alexandrovsk, but no radio contact could be made. During the night, the *Emile Nobel*, escorted by the *Windsor Castle*, sailed back to Petrovsk. The rest of the squadron sailed south and joined the carriers.

It was too late in the day for the CMBs to be used, but the one remaining seaplane on the *Alader Youssanoff* carried out five bombing attacks on Alexandrovsk during 22 May. The pilots reported that a number of sunken ships could be seen. Morrison and Pratt were the crew for two of the raids. After taking off at 05.50 hours, Pratt wrote the following in his log-book:

HMS *Windsor Castle*.

A photograph of the harbour at Alexandrovsk taken on 22 May 1919, showing ships still burning after the attack on 21 May.

Time in Air 50 minutes, Course N E to Alexandrovsk and back, All three bombs 100lbs. to right of ships. Fired on various ships with MG. No AA.[12]

And, later, after taking off at 14.35 hours:

Time in Air 1 hour 25 minutes, Course N E to Alexandrovsk and back, Bombs dropped to right of pier 100Yrds. Fired MG into pier and ships on left of harbour, No AA.[12]

Another armed ship, the *Zoro-Aster*, joined the three other vessels but broke down as soon as it arrived and had to be escorted back to port. This left only two armed British ships, the *Kruger* and *Ventuir*, on station.

Early on 23 May, two Bolshevik destroyers were seen and these opened fire on the British ships from 16,000 yards, well out of range of the British guns. A signal was made by Commodore Norris to the three carriers to disperse out of the way, but Commander Robinson VC, in command of the carriers, hoisted out the seaplane and had two CMBs ready to attack the Red ships when they came in sight. He also ordered smoke to be made. It may be assumed that when the Bolsheviks came under attack from the seaplane and saw the smoke they thought they were being led into an ambush. They turned north and left.

A dense fog closed in across the area and the seaplane crashed while trying to land. British ships rescued the pilot and observer thirty-six hours later, after an extensive search. Nothing was left of the aircraft except one of the floats. The pilot was Sadler, who wrote in his log-book:

Mist had meanwhile come up from southward and was unable to see ships, so sent position by W/T to Youssanoff. Landed on outskirts of fog and taxied from 11.45 till 14.30, when bottom tank was emptied. Then tried to make land by taxying east on top tank; no land sighted by 18.30. Tail float very low in water; wind got up and at 23.30 tailplane, elevator and rudder were wrenched off by swell and machine sunk by stern. An hour later machine turned upside down. Kingham and I clung to floats till 18.30 on the 24th when we were picked up by HMS Asia (Lt. Wilson) 20 miles south-west of Cape Orlok. I had given up hope and was in a pretty rotten state. Asia very decent, gave us hot drinks, hot bath, grub and bed. Arrived Petrovsk 1700, 24th May reported to Commodore.[13]

Information was received that all the remaining Bolshevik ships had left Alexandrovsk and retired to Astrakhan. On 28 May, Commodore Norris left with the *Kruger* to refuel. Captain Washington, with five of the British ships, entered Alexandrovsk and found it deserted. A delegation of the local villagers begged them to stop the bombing. Three barges and twelve other craft were found to have been sunk.

Air reconnaissance showed that most of the Bolshevik fleet had moved up the Volga and was now above Astrakhan. Some of the damaged ships were under repair at the Nobel shipyard, and the RAF kept up the bombing attacks. Commodore Norris received news that the Bolshevik naval commander had been shot and replaced by F. F. Raskolnikov, who had been a petty officer before the Revolution. He had been captured by the British in the Baltic, but had been exchanged for eighteen British prisoners. The eight British armed ships began to patrol the northern half of the Caspian, but no Red ships were seen.

By now, the Air Ministry had decided that it was necessary to replace most of the officers and men sent out with 47 Squadron with volunteers from Britain. Colonel Maund summed up the situation:

Considerable difficulties were experienced, owing to the men being war weary and eager to return home for demobilisation, and Russia in its condition was hardly the place for discontented Men.[14]

It was also thought desirable that an experienced squadron leader should command the squadron. Captain, Acting Major, Raymond Collishaw was asked to take command of the squadron in Russia and to choose the replacement personnel. Collishaw was a Canadian who had shot down at least fifty-eight (possibly sixty-eight) German aircraft during the war, making him the third-ranking Commonwealth air ace. He had commanded 203 Squadron in France and was recognised as one of the RAF's great fighting leaders.

Early in May, Collishaw began to travel around Britain, visiting various airfields to interview men for 47 Squadron:

I left England during the later part of May in Charge of a party of 10 officers and 255 other ranks and after crossing over to Boulogne we boarded a special train that took us to Brindisi, on the heel of Italy. There we boarded a ship that took us through the Dardanelles and on to Constantinople and into the Black Sea.[15]

Collishaw arrived in Novorossisk in early June.

In temporary command of 47 Squadron at Ekaterinodar during May was Captain Sidney G. Frogley. The enormous distances involved in getting about south Russia meant that the main form of transport was the railway. The only practical routes across the steppes were the rail lines and the

Raymond Collishaw, pictured with Muslim tribesmen from the north Caucasus.

rivers, decent roads being few and far between. For 47 Squadron to take part in the fighting, the ground crews, munitions, equipment, spares, and, in some cases, aircraft would have to be moved by rail. It was intended that the squadron would be based on four separate trains, one train for each of the Flights, A, B and C, plus a separate train for the squadron headquarters. With the shortages of rolling stock and engines, it took a considerable time to get the trains together at Ekaterinodar. The Russian railways had a wider gauge than western railways, and a substantial amount of stores could be packed into the carriages. Each of the trains was made up of about fifty trucks. First-class sleeping carriages were provided for the officers, with their own mess, but most of the ground crews slept in bunks placed inside freight cars.

Aircraft could be carried on flat-bed trucks when necessary. Everything that was needed had to be carried on the trains. Getting all this together during the middle of a civil war proved extremely difficult and time consuming. The trains were to be under the nominal command of a Russian air force liaison officer, who would travel with each flight.

Ekaterinodar was a large town, packed with Russian troops. The airfield was two miles outside the town, close to the racetrack, and was known as Chernomorski. During May, temporary hangars were erected to allow the aircraft to be put together after they arrived in crates. Large numbers of

47 Squadron DH9s on the airfield at Ekaterinodar.

Bolshevik prisoners of war were used as labour. These proved to be very reliable and, as long as they were housed, fed, and clothed, gave no trouble. They were, in fact, considered more reliable than the Volunteer Army soldiers. In the railway sidings close to the field, RAF troops struggled to get the trains ready to support the Volunteer Army as it moved forward.

As part of the British Mission to General Denikin, the British had promised to supply the White air force with aircraft. In order to supply these quickly, used aircraft were delivered from RAF units in the Near East. They included Sopwith Camels and DH9s, in addition to at least 100 brand-new RE8s, supplied in crates.

The Russians had great difficulties with the RE8s, as will be described later. In order to train the Russians in the use of the British aircraft, a flying school was set up on the airfield at Ekaterinodar. The intention was to train existing Russian pilots, who may not have flown for some time after the Revolution, and to convert the Russians to the RE8s. It was not intended to carry out *ab initio* training.

The Training Mission as it was initially set up was not a success. Major L. P. Paine was in command of the training section, arriving in Novorossisk with ten officers and fifty-seven other ranks on 26 May. The original instructors were not the best:

> Moreover, four out of the five instructors originally sent out were not suitable, being prisoners of war who had not flown for some time, none of them had flown on RE8s and two of them were seaplane pilots. The fifth had a small experience of RE8s but was not anxious to fly them. None of the 5 were qualified instructors.[16]

Major Paine and the five original instructors had to be replaced in June.

The tank school at Ekaterinodar was able to give the first Russian tank crews only a minimal amount of training, as the tanks were desperately needed at the front line. The tanks first went into action on 8 and 10 May 1919. Describing the action on 10 May, the Russian Major General Agapeev, commanding the tanks, wrote:

> The tanks in this fight made a strong impression on the Reds; the mere sight of the tanks threw the enemy's rank into confusion and he fled panic-stricken abandoning rifles, ammunition and clothing. In general the moral effect of the tanks justified to the full the hopes which were placed in them.[17]

Most of the Red Army had never even seen tanks, let alone had to face them in action.

The first tanks had been rushed into combat, but an attempt was made to give the next wave of tank crews more training. The school that was established at Ekaterinodar ran five-week courses in maintenance, tank driving, and gunnery. All the Russian tank crews were volunteer officers, with no other ranks involved. There are mixed reports on the quality of the Russian officers. Major Bruce was very scathing in his comments on the Russian officers at the tank school, but another officer sent out from Britain to report on the school commented on their keenness and hard work.

The commander of the Russian Tank Corps was Colonel Khaletski, who had been in charge of Russian armoured car units during the First World War. He had visited Britain during 1916 to see the newly developed tanks. Although there were still only twelve tanks operating at the front, their effect was out of proportion to their numbers. Major Sayer described the effect of the Russian tanks:

All whom I interrogated agreed that they could not over estimate the value of the tank in battle, and they told me the effect of the machine upon the enemy was simply 'magical'. It is a fact that, in more than one instance, it has been unnecessary to detrain the tanks since the Bolsheviks bolted at the mere report that a tank train is approaching their positions.[18]

A British Mark V tank shown on a rail flatcar at Novorossisk.

The enormous distances involved in Russia, and the lack of major roads, meant that most of the fighting took place along the rail lines or along the main rivers. Like the air units, the tank units were moved by rail. Most of the Russian troops involved in the fighting were cavalry, and advances and retreats of seventy miles a day were common. The tanks were only used close to the major towns or communications centres where infantry and defensive lines had been deployed.

In some ways, the south Russian countryside was ideal tank country, being flat and well-drained. Major Sayer described the landscape:

> A very large proportion of South Russia consists of the famous 'steppe' country, and one travels thousands of versts, (one verst = two thirds of a mile) for days on end with no relief from the seemingly interminable expanse of dead flat land, usually uncultivated and fit only for grazing purposes ... Large towns are few and far between.[19]

By late May, the twelve tanks at the front were still active, being moved around by train, and the training school was producing the next batch of tank crews as more tanks became available.

NOTES

[1] National Archives , Maund, A. C., report
[2] Knock, D. B., 'An Armourer's Diary', *Popular Flying*, May 1938, page 146
[3] National Archives, 62 Wing diary
[4] Knock, D.B., 'An Armourer's Diary', *Popular Flying*, May 1938, page 148
[5] Ibid.
[6] Ibid.
[7] National Archives, Lynch, John Brayne, log-book
[8] National Archives, 62 Wing diary
[9] Bilney, C. N. H., unpublished memoir
[10] Norris, D., 'Caspian Naval Expedition 1918-1919', *Journal of the Central Asian Society*, Vol. X 1923 part 1, page 228
[11] National Archives, Pratt, H. G., log-book
[12] Ibid.
[13] National Archives, Sadler, J. A., log-book
[14] National Archives, Maund, A. C., report
[15] Collishaw, R., *Air Command*, 1968, William Kimber, London, page 182

[16] National Archives, Holman, H. C., interim report
[17] Agapeev, Major General, 'Weekly Tank Notes No. 48', Royal Tank Corps, 12 July 1919, page 39
[18] Sayer, Major, 'A Visit to the South Russian Tank Corps', *The Tank Corps Journal*, December 1919, page 220
[19] Ibid., page 221

Detail of picture on p. 124.

Detail of picture on p. 56.

CHAPTER TEN

JUNE 1919

By the beginning of June, most of the Armed Forces of South Russia were advancing against the Red Army. On the west flank, the Volunteer Army was advancing into the heart of Russia. The Don Cossack Army was advancing towards Kharkov and the Caucasian Army under Wrangel was continuing its advance towards Tsaritsin. Only the Dagestan Army was bogged down in its attempts to take Astrakhan.

Bad weather, in the form of high wind and mists, was still limiting the attempts by 221 Squadron to bomb Astrakhan. On 1 June, four DH9s from Chechen Island were turned back by bad weather, and, on 3 June, four DH9As from Petrovsk were forced to return after 130 miles. A raid on Astrakhan was successfully carried out on 5 June, however. A floating dock, barges, and oil tanks were bombed and set on fire. Heavy AA fire was experienced. The entire area of the Volga Delta was seen to be flooded, possibly the reason for the slowness of the advance by the Dagestan Army. Although the DH9As searched the Volga for the main Red fleet as far as fifteen miles above Astrakhan, it could not be found. It was thought to have gone farther north, out of the way of the British ships and aircraft. Another raid was carried out from Petrovsk on 7 June.

Besides the raids on Astrakhan, 221 Squadron was also carrying out armed reconnaissance flights in support of the local troops, when weather permitted. On 15 June, a detached flight was established at Grozni as part of the attempt to suppress the local hill tribes. On 16 June, a DH9 from Chechen Island attacked a small armed enemy ship, which was bombed and machine-gunned from low level. The ship was damaged and forced to return to base.

Also on the 16 June, a major raid was mounted on Astrakhan from Petrovsk. At Nobel's yard, two barges containing nine flying boats were seen. These were bombed, and it was claimed that the aircraft were set on fire. A large amount of traffic was seen on the river, but few armed craft were found. Over Astrakhan, one of the DH9As was attacked by a Red air force Nieuport Scout and shot down. The pilot was Second Lieutenant A. J. Mantle and the observer was Second Lieutenant H. Ingram. D. B. Knock recorded in his diary:

> Lieuts. Mantle and Ingram fail to return after raid on Astrakhan. A Flight bombed up for raid and plenty work on C. C. gear and guns. Heard that Mantle and Ingram were attacked by a hostile machine (first one heard of) and driven down. Worked all night and Capt. Grigson kept us going with beer and whisky. Good scout.[1]

Although the two airmen had been shot down, the work continued.

Shooting down a DH9A was a significant achievement as far as the Red pilots were concerned. In Astrakhan, the Red air force had been weakened by the destruction of the flying boat base and of the aircraft on the barges. But they did have available three Nieuport 17s and two Nieuport 25s. They also had a small number of the fighter model of the Sopwith 1½ Strutter. The unit was known as the 47th Reconnaissance Detachment, and was commanded by Mikhail V. Ficher. He had attended pilot training in Britain during the First World War, but was the only member of the unit who was fully trained and had any combat experience. On the first RAF raid on Astrakhan, naval pilot Stoyarov had taken off in a Nieuport, but had never seen the British aircraft. During the raid on 5 May, S. G. Kalan and Ficher took off but, again, the RAF aircraft were not seen. The Nieuports were in poor condition, mainly because of the extremely low quality of the aviation fuel they were forced to use. Because of the conditions and the shortage of mechanics and spare parts, the life of new military aircraft during the Russian Civil War was thought of as just three months, after which the aircraft were judged to be worn out.

Early in June, two more pilots were sent down to Astrakhan from Moscow. These two were both recent graduates of the Moscow Flying School. Although they lacked combat experience, the two had at least received adequate training. Their names were D. N. Shchekin and A. P. Korotkov, and they were classified as naval pilots. The early experience with the British raids had shown that it was nearly impossible to intercept the faster DH9As by waiting until the raids had been detected and then taking off. The only alternative was to mount standing patrols. Because of the small numbers of pilots and aircraft, plus the state of the aircraft themselves, the patrols can only have been patchy at best.

Nevertheless, on 16 June, Shchekin and Korotkov, flying in Nieuport 17s, saw four DH9As flying towards them at a height of 2,100 metres and

Left: D. N. Shchekin. Right: A. P. Korotkov. This is claimed to be the wreckage of the DH9A shot down by Shchekin close to Astrakhan on 16 June 1919.

carried out a frontal attack. Shchekin hit one of the DH9As in the radiator and the aircraft was seen to be trailing steam. The engine overheated and burned out. Mantle and Ingram landed safely in a cultivated field twenty miles south-east of Astrakhan. The two British aircrew set fire to their aircraft and tried to escape across the countryside, but were captured by Red cavalry and sent north to Moscow. They were held as prisoners of war in Moscow until they were repatriated on 31 March 1920; Ingram reported to the Air Ministry on 24 April 1920. As a reward, Shchekin was given a bonus of 5,000 roubles. Shchekin claimed to have shot down a second RAF aircraft later in the month, but there is absolutely no evidence in RAF files of a second aircraft being shot down.

There was another raid on Astrakhan on 19 June, by aircraft from Petrovsk. In retaliation for the aircraft lost on 16 June, the DH9As attacked the Red airfield, as detailed in the Wing diary:

> Aerodrome S. E. of railway station. Three sheds in line at the east end; three machines on ground and one in the air, which was attacked hit and forced to descend.[2]

Shipping and barges on the river were also bombed. The Russian records claim that no aircraft were lost to 221 Squadron, but the records are at best incomplete and there was a definite policy of not admitting losses. It is also claimed by the Russians that aircraft from 221 Squadron only carried out bombing attacks from 12,000 ft after the loss of the aircraft on 16 June, but squadron records speak about the attacking aircraft carrying

221 Squadron DH9As.

out machine-gun attacks from low level. Nobody carries out machine-gun attacks from 12,000 ft.

The command of 221 Squadron passed to Major Gordon on 21 June. A major attack was mounted on Astrakhan on 27 June, with eight aircraft dropping two and a half tons of bombs. Shipping was again bombed and machine-gunned, plus:

> Aerodrome and vicinity – five machines; two attacked and were driven down ... Aerodrome, workshops hit, owing to close fall of bombs, must have been damaged, also shot up by machine guns. Aerodrome badly holed. Machines on aerodrome, namely two, attacked from 100 feet and shot up. Volga is decreasing in flood; country around Astrakhan again above water.[3]

The term 'driven down' was used in these reports to describe the fate of several Red air force aircraft that attacked the DH9As. This term was used during the First World War, and there is now much discussion as to what was really meant by the term. Does it mean the aircraft was destroyed, damaged, probably damaged, or just driven off? It is hard to tell. No individual claims to have destroyed enemy aircraft were made by the pilots of 221 Squadron. The Russians claim that no aircraft were lost. Lieutenant Gayford was in no doubt that Russian aircraft were destroyed:

Astrakhan and the Bolshevik flotilla in the Volga delta was our real objective, and numerous bomb raids were carried out on these targets. A. A. fire over Astrakhan was increasing in volume and accuracy, and the enemy was sending up quite a number of aircraft to engage us. We had shot several of them down and lost one aircraft ourselves.[4]

How many he meant by 'several' is hard to say.

Bad weather stopped any more major raids during the month, but demonstration and reconnaissance flights continued. A flight was detached from 221 Squadron during the month to operate from an advanced landing strip at Lagan, which had been captured by the White troops. This flight was attached to the Army attacking Astrakhan and strafed enemy troops with machine-gun fire. Messages were also passed between the different White Army columns by the aircraft landing on the steppes close by:

> The machines working with General Dratzenka are doing very well. They have to land three or four times each flight at any emergency landing ground close to the troops in order to give them information as to the whereabouts of the enemy and also their own troops.[5]

From the middle of May, the 5th Air Detachment of the Volunteer Army, under the command of Lieutenant Zavodsk, had also been operating from Petrovsk. This unit had been operating SPAD 7s, Nieuports, and Morane 4s, but as 221 received more DH9As they passed their DH9s on to the 5th Detachment. It is claimed that this unit also carried out shipping strikes on the Caspian and raids on Astrakhan, after refuelling at Chechen Island. More DH9As were received by 221 during June. D. B. Knock wrote in his diary:

> 22/6/19 six more 9 Acks arrive from Baku ... Hear that Jack Alcock, late of Mudros, has flown across the Atlantic.
> 24/6/19 News that peace is signed. Much talk of going home in consequence. Too hot to breathe so swam around in oily Caspian. Winged pests are terrible to contend with. Burned bushes near tent with petrol to settle a few. Found they had merely settled inside walls of tent in millions.[6]

The conditions do not seem to have got any better.

During the month, another volunteer arrived in Petrovsk This was Lieutenant Vic Clow. He had learned to fly in Egypt during the war, and had gone on to fly escort missions over the Suez Canal. In London after the war, he had volunteered to serve in Russia.

One flight of 266 Squadron continued to operate on the seaplane carrier, while the other operated from shore bases at Petrovsk and Chechen. Captain Bilney flew one of the seaplanes north to Chechen Island, with one other aircraft. They were stranded there for nearly two weeks, as Bilney later recalled:

> Apart from our crews of three officers and an Airman Gunner, there was one other Airman on this lonely sandbank, used by a few fishermen whose main catch was big Sturgeon. The Airman's job was to look after the fuel supplies and attend to any aeroplanes which used the rough landing strip occasionally.[7]

The seaplanes flew short reconnaissances along the coast, but the weather restricted their distance. At the best of times, the performance of the Short 184s was only marginal, and rough sea stopped them from taking off. After several days of the monotonous diet on Chechen, the resident airman produced succulent fried sturgeon steaks he had bought off the fishermen. The next day, Bilney found out that they had been fried in engine oil. The seaplanes continued to fly reconnaissance patrols whenever the weather allowed.

Captain Sadler was still commanding the seaplane flight on the *Alader Youssanoff*. Early in the month, a convoy to Guryev on the Ural River,

266 Squadron aircrew on board HMS *Alader Youssanoff* during May 1919.

which was the HQ of the Ural Cossacks, was escorted by the British ships. Reconnaissance flights over Fort Alexandrovsk were carried out on 12 June, but no Red ships were seen. A landing by White troops ensured that the Red navy would not use Alexandrovsk again. On 17 June, the crew of a Red air force flying boat from Astrakhan defected to the British, landing on the water close to one of the British ships. It was hoisted in and later handed over to the White Russians, who used it to bomb Astrakhan. Because of engine difficulties, the seaplane carrier's top speed had been getting slower and slower, so between 13 and 18 June the *Alader Youssanoff* put into Petrovsk to have her boilers cleaned.

On 24 June, the ship was back at sea in the north Caspian, and the two seaplanes carried out a reconnaissance of the mouth of the Volga. A paddle steamer, three tugs, and one motor launch were bombed and machine-gunned. Two bombing raids were carried out on the coast of Lagan on 25 June. On 26 June, the seaplane carrier anchored off Chechen Island. A reconnaissance by two machines did not find any thing worth bombing. Another reconnaissance was carried out on 27 June. The Wing diary for 28 June reads:

> One machine being unable to get off the water owing to swell dropped one 112 lb. bomb to lighten herself. Bomb exploded, and blew the machine in half. Pilot and Observer slightly injured. Machine complete loss. Evening patrol of 12 ft. anchorage. Nothing to report.[8]

The lost aircraft was number N9082.

During the month of June, General Wrangel continued to advance against the 10th Red Army in the direction of Tsaritsin. With its position on the Volga, Tsaritsin had always been a strategic and trading centre. Timber was brought down the river from the forests in the north, and products were brought from the Middle East across the Caspian and north along the Volga to Tsaritsin. It had also become an industrial centre, with the population growing to around 120,000 in 1919. After the Revolution, Tsaritsin was run by a Soviet committee that at one time included Stalin, along with Vorishilov and Budenny (both of whom later attained the rank of marshal of the Red Army). Stalin had controlled the defence of the town during 1918, when the Don Cossacks had tried to take it. He considered this to be his moment of triumph, which was why he renamed the place Stalingrad in 1925. However, by June 1919, Stalin had gone elsewhere and the Red Army commander in the area was a former Tsarist officer, General Kluiev, the commander of the 10th Red Army.

For the 200-mile advance to Tsaritsin, Wrangel had three cavalry corps, one brigade of dismounted Cossacks, and the under-strength 6th Infantry

Division under his command. During the Russian Civil War, many of the units on both sides were only nominally up to strength, and some of the corps involved comprised as few as 1,500 men. All the bridges and viaducts on the rail line to Tsaritsin had been destroyed, slowing the White Army's advance. This area of Russia has little water, and the horses and men had great difficulty finding supplies, as did Hitler's troops twenty-three years later.

One of Wrangel's cavalry corps, commanded by General Pokrovsky, advanced along the rail line to Tsaritsin. Another corps, commanded by General Ulagai, was on the right wing and a third corps, under General Chatilov, was in the rear as a reserve. The Red Army unexpectedly counter-attacked along the rail line. The 6th Infantry Division was overrun by Red cavalry and infantry and was nearly destroyed. General Ulagai managed to attack the Red forces on their left wing, driving them back. By 11 June, Wrangel's forces had reached the outer defences of Tsaritsin. Surrounding Tsaritsin were two lines of trenches, one at a distance of ten miles and one close to the outskirts of the town.

Great efforts were made to open up the rail line back to the White headquarters at Ekaterinodar to bring up supplies and reinforcements for the White forces outside Tsaritsin. These forces were never large enough to cut off the city completely and the Red Army continued to move men and

The port of Novorossisk. Most of the equipment for 47 Squadron and the British Military Mission came in through this port.

equipment into the town. A large flotilla of riverboats was also brought north from Astrakhan by the Reds. The River Volga was over a mile wide at Tsaritsin, and these gunboats provided a mobile artillery reserve for the Red Army. Wrangel decided he would have to take the town before reinforcements could reach him, as the Bolshevik forces in Tsaritsin were growing stronger each day.

On 6 June, the SS *War Celt* arrived in Novorossisk with more equipment and personnel for 47 Squadron. Major Collishaw arrived in the port of Novorossisk on 8 June and officially took over command from Captain Frogley on 13 June. For the next few weeks, Collishaw remained at Novorossisk carrying out administrative work and attempting to reorganise the supply situation in the port. On 10 June, C Flight left Ekaterinodar to support Wrangel's forces. Commanding C Flight was Captain H. G. Davies, one of the original 47 Squadron flight commanders. Captain Davies was described by the historian H. A. Jones, who had known him in Salonika:

> He was one of the original observers of 47 Squadron joining the squadron in its early days in Salonika. He did excellent work over the Vardar front and was often chosen for the most difficult jobs. After a spell on that front he went to Egypt and qualified as a pilot. He returned to the squadron in 1918. He was a quiet, intense, stout hearted officer. He was sound rather than brilliant, and much of the fine work done by 'C' Flight in South Russia can be traced back to his example.[9]

The flight was made up of five DH9s, all of which had already seen considerable use.

The train went ahead to Velikoknyajeskaya, 180 miles north-east of Ekaterinodar, with Lieutenant Grigorieff in nominal command. There were many areas that could be used as landing fields on the flat rolling steppes, and once the train had pulled off the track into sidings at a suitable place the aircraft could land and join the train. Early in the morning of 10 June, the five DH9s left Ekaterinodar. Four of the aircraft arrived safely, but one made a forced landing in a field only twenty miles from Ekaterinodar. A party was sent out under the control of Lieutenant Dumas; the wings were taken off the aircraft and it was brought back to Ekaterinodar on the railway.

On 12 June, the train moved forward another fifty-five miles, to Zimovnika. As the rail line was the main supply route for Baron Wrangel's army, it was extremely congested and the move took thirteen hours. The four aircraft were successfully flown up to join the train. Captain Davies was promised that the bridges would soon be repaired, but the Army at the

C Flight, pictured at Beketovka. Front row, second from left: Lieutenant Simmons.
Middle row, left: Lieutenant Grigorieff (?), -?-, Captain Frogley, Major Collishaw,
Captain Anderson, -?-, Captain Elliot. Back row: -?-, Captain Hatchett, -?-,
Lieutenant Mitchell.

front was in need of food and supplies so the first trains across would have
to be the Army trains. Without the rail line, the only transport on the other
side of the bridge, to the fighting at Tsaritsin, was by horse. Over the next
two days, no flying was possible because of heavy rainstorms and wind.
Captain Davies seems to have been disappointed with his experience of
dealing with the Russians, commenting in the squadron diary that 'they
promise everything but rarely carry out anything at all'.

On the afternoon of 15 June, the first bridge was finally opened and
C Flight's train passed over just after midnight. The train arrived at
Kotelnokovo during the afternoon of 16 June. When the four DH9s
arrived at the area chosen as the airfield, one of them crashed on landing.
Bad weather stopped any chance of flying over the next two days. On
19 June, the DH9 that had made a forced landing on 10 June arrived at
Kotelnokovo, flown by Lieutenant White, with Lieutenant Webb as his
observer, after being repaired at Ekaterinodar.

General Wrangel's three cavalry corps were not the ideal troops for
a frontal attack on prepared positions, but on 14 June a major attack
was launched on the western side of the town. The attack was renewed
on 15 June, but the Reds were able to concentrate armoured trains

with heavy artillery to bombard the attackers. Without proper infantry support, the attack was doomed to failure. During the offensive, five divisional commanders, three brigade commanders, and eleven regimental commanders were killed or wounded.

After this severe setback, Wrangel was forced to wait for reinforcements. Part of the promised reinforcements were the 7th Infantry Division, three armoured trains, five batteries of guns, aircraft from 47 Squadron RAF, and six tanks. On 16 June, four tanks from the 2nd and the 4th Sections of the Russian Tank Corps, along with two tanks from the training school at Ekaterinodar, were dispatched to the Tsaritsin front. The only part of the British Military Mission that was officially intended to take part in the fighting was 47 Squadron.

The second bridge was repaired on 20 June, and C Flight's train moved forward to Gniloaksaiskaya, within sixty miles of Tsaritsin. Another crash occurred when Lieutenant Clavey was landing close to the train. C Flight had finally arrived within operating distance of Tsaritsin, but only had three aircraft ready for use. On the day after C Flight arrived, the Red forces counter-attacked and forced the White forces back to within ten miles of C Flight's airfield. A first operation was mounted on 22 June, with four aircraft (one of the damaged aircraft having been repaired), but this was forced to turn back through bad weather and one aircraft crashed on landing, reducing the number of serviceable aircraft back to three.

On 23 June, three DH9s carried out the first successful operation, as recorded in the squadron diary:

Three machines left at 1030 hours with 16–20 lbs and 2–112 lbs bombs and bombed Tsaritsin. Height 5000'. Objective was S. E. railway station. Damage done to station buildings, rolling stock and neighbouring houses, 1,000 rounds S. A. A. were fired into barges on VOLGA, station, streets and cavalry near ELSHANKA.[10]

The pilots were Captain Davies, Lieutenant White, and Lieutenant Verity. Tsaritsin was bombed again, by three aircraft, on 24 June and once more, by two aircraft, on 25 June.

By 22 June, the first elements of the 7th Infantry Division arrived at Tsaritsin. They were equipped with British uniforms and rifles. Wrangel concentrated his forces on his right wing against the River Volga. On the far right, was the Cossack Infantry Brigade. Next to them was the 7th Infantry Division. Behind the infantry were two of Wrangel's cavalry corps, waiting to exploit any breakthrough. The other corps was positioned to cut off any Red Army troops who tried to escape to the north. Behind the front line were the tanks and three armoured cars. It was believed that as

The railway station at Tsaritsin. The station was bombed during June 1919 by 47 Squadron but the damage does not seem to be extensive.

many as 40,000 Red Army troops were in the town, with over a hundred guns, six armoured trains, and a number of gunboats on the river.

Another DH9 was sent forward to C Flight from Ekaterinodar on 26 June. Lieutenant Watson flew this aircraft, Lieutenant Addison having flown him back to Ekaterinodar as a passenger in order to pick the aircraft up. Lieutenant Watson, however, only arrived at the front on 30 June after suffering a forced landing on the way. Also on 26 June, two sorties were carried out against Tsaritsin in the morning, followed by another three sorties against transport targets north of Tsaritsin in the afternoon. C Flight was operating 340 miles away from its headquarters at Ekaterinodar; on 27 June a DH9 flown by Lieutenants Verity and Thompson flew the distance to the Ekaterinodar HQ in three hours and twenty minutes. On the same day, Major Bruce, who was commanding the British tanks, was taken up as an observer in a DH9 flown by Lieutenant White in order to view the lines at Tsaritsin. The Reds had positioned an observation balloon close to the point of attack, enabling Red observers to see the movement of the tanks. This balloon was attacked by Major Bruce and Lieutenant White and forced to descend. On 28 June, one sortie was mounted in the morning and another in the afternoon. A 20 lb bomb hit a tug on the River Volga.

One RAF aircraft was allocated for co-operation with the tanks and a code of signals was arranged. Wrangel appointed Major Bruce as overall commander of the tanks and the date of the attack was set for 29 June. One of the Mk V tanks had broken down, leaving two Mk Vs and three

Whippets for the assault. The British tank officers were under orders from the British government not to become involved in the fighting, but Major Bruce ignored the order and allowed one tank to be crewed by British troops under the command of Captain Walsh.

On the night before the battle, a White Russian cavalry officer, Captain Petrov, was waiting outside Tsaritsin, as he later recalled:

> I suddenly remembered that I had had nothing to eat the previous day. I saw some men pulling a boat ashore and wandered over to them. They were fishermen. Thrashing about in the bottom of the boat was a large sturgeon. 'How about some caviar, Captain?' one of the fishermen called out. Taking a knife he slit open the fish and a mass of black caviar oozed out. Spreading some on a piece of black bread, he offered it to me ... This was fifty years ago, but whenever I get to eat caviar, I still see before me the Volga, the receding darkness, the fishermen and the sturgeon: I almost feel again that mixture of hunger and fear that gnawed at me then, on the eve of the great battle of Tsaritsin.[11]

Wrangel's plan was for the tanks to break through the Red Army trench line, supported by the infantry, and for the cavalry to pass through to take the town. Supplies of petrol, oil, and grease for the tanks were to be brought up by bullock cart, with one cart allocated to each tank.

At 02.00 hours on 29 June, the tanks began to move forward from their start line. One of the three Whippets had broken down, leaving only two for the attack. The two Mk V tanks crossed the front line at 02.30 hours, followed by the two Whippets. The tanks came under heavy machine-gun fire, which had no effect. As planned, the British-crewed tank turned left after crossing the trench line and began to move forward behind the trenches, firing into them and breaking down the wire. The second in command of the British tank, Captain McElvaine, described the battle:

> On approaching the line, the tanks came under pretty heavy rifle and Machine gun fire for 10–15 minutes, but, as the tanks came near the enemy retired rapidly ... the other Mk. V went to the assistance of a Whippet which had got caught in the wire.[12]

The Russian-crewed tanks fired into the retreating Red Army troops. The British tank turned north towards the town of Tsaritsin after moving behind the Bolshevik lines for five miles. At 05.30 hours, Captain Walsh was injured by a shell splinter after he had left the tank to talk to one of the White Russian infantry commanders and Captain McElvaine assumed command of the tank. For some reason, the Russian tanks had returned to the starting point, but they were ordered forward again by Major Bruce. The Russian armoured cars had followed the tanks through the gap they had created in the trench line and moved forward to attack Tsaritsin from the west. The rallying point for the tanks was at Beketofskaya, south-west of the town.

By 12.00 hours, three tanks – the two Mk Vs and one Whippet, the other Whippet having broken down – were at the rallying point and had been refuelled and armed by the bullock carts that had followed them forward. At 15.00 hours, Major Bruce gave the order to advance on Tsaritsin. The Red Army had a second line of defences around the outskirts of the town and most of the defenders had retreated to their second line. Advancing behind the retreating defenders, the White forces had stopped outside the town. Just as the three tanks arrived at 17.00 hours, the Bolsheviks launched a major counter-attack south along the bank of the Volga, supported by artillery mounted on the gunboats.

Colonel Tseshks, the commanding officer of the 1st Russian Tank Division, described this action:

> At 5 o'clock in the afternoon the tanks rallied at Voroponovo station, and from this point moved against Tsaritsin from the South in order to assist our right flank which was being pressed by the Reds. Here under heavy artillery fire from both land and river, they restored the position of our troops on the right and caused the Reds to retire into the town.[13]

Although the Red counter-attack was defeated, the heavy artillery fire did damage two of the tanks. Captain McElvaine, in the British-crewed tank, recorded what happened:

> Whilst running along a ridge towards Tsaritsin the machines came under heavy fire from about 12 guns of, I believe 4" calibre, firing over open sights. The Whippet was hit by a shell splinter, which broke 2 engine holding down bolts, and one Mk. V developed ignition trouble.[14]

Major Bruce ordered the tanks to pull back a safe distance from the fighting for the night, which they spent in a ravine two miles south of Tsaritsin.

On 29 June, three aircraft from C Flight left extremely early in the morning, at 03.20 hours, to bomb Tsaritsin, and returned at 05.00 hours after hitting troop and transport targets. Later in the day, two more aircraft bombed the Tsaritsin area, while at 08.30 two more sorties were laid on. In the afternoon, Lieutenants Clavey and Hopwood flew a reconnaissance. This showed that the Red Army was starting to retreat in a north-easterly direction along the river.

At the end of the first day's fighting, the Red forces had pulled back into the town of Tsaritsin and had abandoned the outer defence line. The war diary for C Flight 47 Squadron on 29 June reads:

> The enemy was observed in Gumrak area retreating in a N. E. direction. In the morning at 04.00 hrs enemy was observed evacuating his front line trenches and all his transport was retreating at full speed along roads and open country towards Gumrak and Elshanka. In the evening the Volunteer Army occupied the line Elshanka–Grutenka.[15]

It was arranged that the two remaining Mk V tanks would go into action at 02.00 hours on 30 June, but no supplies of petrol could be obtained. The bullock carts had vanished. Either they had been commandeered by other units or the drivers had decided that following tanks in open carts was not the safest occupation. White troops again attacked the town on the morning of 30 June. Red Army units were holding buildings along the streets and causing heavy casualties with rifle and machine-gun fire. The 3rd Kuban Cossack Division, fighting on foot, and the 7th Infantry Division fought their way into the town along the bank of the river.

By 19.00 hours, the tanks had finally been refuelled and, with Major Bruce in command of the British-crewed tank, the two tanks advanced into the streets of Tsaritsin. By this time, the Red Army defenders had broken and a mass retreat to the north was under way. Wrangel claimed to have captured 40,000 prisoners, 300 machine-guns, several armoured trains, and an enormous stock of supplies when Tsaritsin fell. The remains of the Red Army retreated north along the Volga River to Kamyshin, followed by the advancing White Army. But Wrangel's forces were too exhausted to follow up the Red defeat at Tsaritsin with any effectiveness.

Only one unit had represented the Red air force in Tsaritsin, the 7th Fighter Detachment. This unit had been moved into the area in the middle of May and was based on the airfield at Beketovka, just south of Tsaritsin. White air force aircraft began to bomb the city early in June, but none of them were intercepted by the 7th Fighter Detachment. The Detachment had five Nieuport fighters on its strength early in the month, but two of these collided while taxiing. On 10 June, the remaining three Nieuports were ordered back to Kamyshin, farther north on the Volga, but two of the aircraft crashed when landing at the airfield. The 4th Fighter Detachment arrived in Tsaritsin on 24 June with four aircraft. This unit carried out ten sorties before being forced to retire on 29 June. One White Russian Nieuport was claimed to have been shot down on 28 June; the pilot survived the crash but was killed by Red Army troops.

More RAF personnel began to arrive in south Russia during the month. Lieutenant A. P. Ritchie had volunteered and was transferred from Egypt:

> On arrival I found that I was not wanted in Georgia but that there was an RAF detachment of some sort at Novorossisk. I took the first boat going there and arrived to find the detachment consisted of approximately two flights of 47 Squadron. The two flights moved to Ekaterinodar, the headquarters of the RAF mission and I remained in charge of the port base for the next six weeks, an occupation for which I had no liking. On the arrival of an RAF training unit from England, I handed over my duties at Novorossisk and joined 47 Squadron at Ekaterinodar ... The RAF training unit was in a nasty predicament. They had found their Headquarters and settled down only to discover that they had brought no pilots who could fly the RE8s with which they were equipped, and no mechanics who knew anything about this type of aircraft; so none had been erected. Volunteers were called for from 47 squadron. I had nothing to do so I applied.[16]

It took some while for the training flight to recover from the original poor choice of personnel.

Captain Walter Anderson was to become one of the stalwarts of 47 Squadron. Anderson arrived in the Black Sea port of Novorossisk on 25 June. He described the train journey from the Black Sea to Ekaterinodar:

A DH9A belonging to 47 Squadron, shown on the ground at Ekaterinodar.

The train was packed. I had never before seen a train so crowded, people were hanging on everywhere; they were even on the roof.[17]

When he arrived in Ekaterinodar, Captain Anderson had an interview with General Kravtseyvitch, the Russian general in command of the White air force. Anderson was promised the command of a Russian squadron, but after three weeks he found out that the existing commander had refused to step down and he was now expected to be joint commander. This he refused, and he became one of 47 Squadron's pilots. During the month of June, 47 Squadron had flown 100 hours and 30 minutes.

One of the stories told about 47 Squadron during the capture of Tsaritsin involved the killing of a number of Soviet commissars. The truth of this incident is hard to judge. J. E. Hodgson referred to it when he visited Tsaritsin several months after the capture of the city:

> Before he had captured Tsaritsin news came through to Vrangel [sic] that a conference of Bolshevik Commissars, which eighty of the Soviet leaders were expected to attend, had been convened at the Soviet buildings. A DH9 went up carrying a British pilot and a 112lb. Bomb. It circled round the town, defying the enemy guns, identified the meetinghouse, and dropped the huge missile of death upon it. Not a single Commissar could have escaped alive. I subsequently found the site, but very few signs of the building itself.[18]

Collishaw also mentions the incident with the commissars in his book *Air Command*:

> On one raid that the flight flew against Czaritsyn [sic] it dropped a 112-pound bomb squarely on a building in which the local Soviet was holding a full session. All but two of the 41 Red officials were killed.[19]

No mention of the incident can be found in the official records. Neither Hodgson nor Collishaw were present in the area before the fall of Tsaritsin, or just after, and this story may not be accurate.

During June, General Briggs was replaced by Major General H. C. Holman as the leader of the British Military Mission in south Russia. Holman had been a brigade commander during the First World War. He was a tall, impressive-looking man who believed in leading from the front.

NOTES

1 D. B. Knock, 'An Armourer's Diary', *Popular Flying*, May 1938, page 148
2 National Archives, 62 Wing diary
3 Ibid.
4 National Archives, Gayford, O. R., War Experiences
5 National Archives, 62 Wing diary
6 Knock, D. B., 'An Armourer's Diary', *Popular Flying*, May 1938, page 148
7 Bilney, C. N. H., unpublished memoir
8 National Archives, 62 Wing diary
9 Jones, H. A., *Over the Balkans and South Russia, Being the Story of No. 47 Squadron RAF*, 1923
10 National Archives, 47 Squadron diary
11 Quoted in Wrangel, A., *General Wrangel 1878-1929 Russia's White Crusader*, Leo Cooper, London, 1987, page 108-09
12 McElvane, Captain, 'Weekly Tank Notes No. 62', Royal Tank Corps, October 1919
13 Tseshks, Colonel, 'Reports of the 1st Division of Russian Tank Corps', Weekly Tank Notes, Royal Tank Corps, October 1919
14 McElvane, Captain, 'Weekly Tank Notes No. 62', Royal Tank Corps, October 1919
15 National Archives, 47 Squadron diary
16 National Archives, Ritchie, A. P., War Experiences
17 National Archives, Anderson, W. F., War Experiences
18 Hodgson, J. E., *With Denikin's Armies*, London, 1932, page 142-43
19 Collishaw, R., *Air Command*, William Kimber, London, 1972, page 184

CHAPTER ELEVEN

JULY 1919

After the capture of Tsaritsin, General Denikin visited the town on 2 July. While he was there, he issued what was to become known as the Moscow Directive. His overall plan was that all the troops of the Armed Forces of South Russia should advance towards Moscow. This would involve advances of 400 miles for the Volunteer Army and the Don Army and an advance of 750 miles for the Caucasian Army under Wrangel. Denikin said that he would only need the small-scale maps for this advance. Wrangel thought this scheme was completely beyond the abilities of the forces Denikin had under his command. When he told Denikin this, there was a major disagreement between the two. But Denikin insisted and Wrangel, following orders, advanced north along the Volga and captured Kamyshin on 28 July. Most of Wrangel's heavy forces were transferred to the central front; his Cossack forces were exhausted through heavy fighting and the distances travelled.

The Volunteer Army under General Mai-Maevsky continued to advance northward towards Moscow and captured Kharkov on 25 July. In the centre, the Don Cossack Army under General Sidorin also continued its northward advance. Only General Erdel and the Dagestan Army were not advancing; they were still stalled in their attempts to take Astrakhan. On 1 July, the flight from 221 Squadron that was attached to the Dagestan Army carried out a bombing attack on four Red Navy paddle steamers forty miles north-east of Lagan. Describing the work of the detached flight, the Wing diary states:

> They have had to work out in the open with no facilities for repairs etc. and both officers and men have had a hard time. On July 1st they were forced to evacuate Lagan in a hurry owing to the advance of the Bolshevik Army.[1]

From Petrovsk, the local reconnaissance and demonstration flights continued. On 7 July, one DH9 from Chechen Island was hit by enemy fire while attacking shipping. The observer was injured and the aircraft was forced to land on the way back to Chechen. The aircraft could not be repaired and was burned.

On 9 July, a raid was carried out on Astrakhan. One large armed barge was bombed and machine-gunned, even though it put up severe AA fire. A paddle steamer was bombed and set on fire. No aircraft were seen on the aerodromes, but two Nieuports were seen on the ground in a field. On the way back, one machine suffered engine failure and had to carry out a forced landing. Luckily, this was on the right side of the lines. Another raid on Astrakhan was carried out on 10 July. Shipping in the River Volga was again attacked. Oil tanks were set on fire, with the smoke rising to 8,000 feet. Further action was detailed in the diary:

> Barges off Admiralty Point also hit. Attacked by Six enemy aircraft; these were engaged and driven down.[2]

Six aircraft is more than the entire number of fighter aircraft that the Red air force claimed to have in the area. One of the DH9As again had to force land on the way back inside friendly territory. This aircraft was repaired and returned to Petrovsk by 19 July.

The crews of machines stationed at Petrovsk began to report that they were being fired on whenever they over flew any of the local villages. This was always put down to Bolshevik agitators, but the situation was much more complex than that. The whole area of the Caucasus was, and still is, a mix of opposed ethnic and religious groups. There was strong support for the Reds but also support for local nationalists. General Denikin was seen, rightly or wrongly, as representing a return to the old ways. Support for the British was very thin on the ground. Local villages that did fire on the British aircraft were bombed and machine-gunned. In addition, aircraft from Chechen Island bombed ships in the mouth of the Volga on 13 July.

Four DH9As carried out a raid on Astrakhan on 17 July. Shipping and store sheds were bombed. No enemy aircraft were seen. Local villages were bombed on 21 and 24 July by aircraft from Petrovsk, and a raid on Astrakhan was mounted by DH9As on 25 July. The main Red fleet could still not be found, but one Finn class destroyer was seen. Shipping in the river was bombed and a store shed was also demolished. The Wing diary noted that:

> The presence at Mogilny of a Finn class destroyer shows that the reports of deserters from Astrakhan are not quite correct. They reported all Finn

class destroyers to have gone above Tsaritsin ... The bombing of the
hostile villages has had excellent effect and they have now practically all
been taken by General Popoff's troops ... The work at 221 Squadron has
been seriously interfered with owing to the prevalence of local fever.[3]

On 27 July, two machines set out to bomb Mogilny but were forced to
turn back because of heavy haze. Two aircraft were again detached on 31
July to support the Army trying to advance on Astrakhan.

The *Alader Youssanoff* was anchored off Chechen Island early in the
month. Two aircraft from 266 Squadron carried out a reconnaissance
of the mouth of the Volga on 5 July, but nothing was seen. Another
reconnaissance was undertaken on 7 July, but again nothing was seen. The
overall performance of the *Alader Youssanoff* had deteriorated to the point
where she could only manage five knots. Commodore Norris, in command
of the British ships, agreed to the CMB depot ship *Orlionoch* becoming
the new seaplane carrier. The guns and equipment were transferred from
the *Alader Youssanoff* to the *Orlionoch* in the port at Petrovsk. The new
carrier sailed on 17 July, carrying two Short 184s.

Orlionoch anchored off Seal Island on 18 July and launched the two
aircraft on a raid to Lagan. No targets were seen and the aircraft became
lost in mist on the return trip. Captain Sadler and Lieutenant McCughey,
the two pilots, beached their aircraft on the coast and spent the night in
a fisherman's cottage. In the morning, they returned to the carrier. On 21
July, the ship had moved to the east coast of the sea and both machines
carried out a patrol, but again nothing was seen. The *Orlionoch* was
in company with the CMB carrier, and a patrol was flown on 22 July,
escorting the two CMBs in a reconnaissance along the coast.

On 24 July, the *Orlionoch* was again anchored off Seal Island on the west
coast and launched the two aircraft for a reconnaissance of the mouth of
the Volga and Lagan. Captain Sadler, with Lieutenant J. W. Turton-Jones
as his observer, flew one of the aircraft. Nothing was seen at Lagan but
then a seaborne target presented itself:

Off Lighthouse, armed tug observed approaching; this was attacked by
bombs, no direct hits obtained. Machines then came down to 800 feet
and engaged tug with machine guns with apparently good effect. One
machine [Sadler's aircraft] badly hit in engine and forced to land 15
miles away from lighthouse. The other machine also was shot about.
One machine escorted C.M.B's, proceeding to pick up damaged seaplane.
Seaplane found and position given. C.M.B's picked up and towed
seaplane to ship.[4]

Russian authorities claim this Short 184 as being shot down by the Red Navy. There is no doubt that it was shot down, but it was recovered and hoisted back on board the *Orlionoch* at 14.30 hours.

Captain Bilney sailed from Petrovsk on board the *Orlionoch* on 27 July. The ship was heading for the north-east corner of the Caspian, where the Ural River runs into the sea. A few miles inland on the river is the town of Guryev, then the headquarters of the Ural Cossacks. With Bilney were two Short 184s, three other officers, and maintenance personnel. The intention was to hand over the two aircraft to the Cossacks, after they had been instructed on their use and maintenance. As it was impossible for the ship to get close to Guryev because of shallow water, at thirty miles offshore the two aircraft were launched to fly up the River Ural to Guryev. When they contacted the local Russians, Bilney and his men found that nobody was expecting them, nobody wanted to fly the aircraft, and nobody could speak English.

The Russian flying service in the area had an airfield with two Farman biplanes and one Nieuport, as well as one small flying boat on the river. A Russian pilot, Captain Igoroff, was finally persuaded to fly Bilney's seaplane. After several hours' instruction, Igoroff, who was described by Bilney as a competent and confident pilot, went solo in the Short. The following day, Igoroff flew the Short on bombing raids on the front line south of Astrakhan, with a Russian mechanic serving as his observer. Igoroff refused to use bomb racks and insisted that the observer carry the bombs in his cockpit and throw them out by hand. For two days, Igoroff successfully bombed the front line. On the third day, Bilney watched him take off and vanish in a mid-air explosion:

> So ended our instructional duties, for none of the other Russians wanted to fly, and when we eventually departed our one remaining seaplane was left, together with spares, presumably to rot.[5]

The party of RAF men sampled the hospitality of the Cossacks at first hand and developed a liking for the local vodka. Bilney and the rest of his airmen eventually returned to Petrovsk in August.

At the start of July, C Flight was still operating from the village of Gniloaksaiskaya, south of Tsaritsin. After the capture of the city, the fighting moved north-east along the Volga and north-west towards the Don River. Several attempts were made to carry out a reconnaissance on 1 July, but bad weather forced the aircraft back. On 2 July, Lieutenants Clavey and Hopwood attacked barges on the Volga that were being used by Red Army troops during their retreat. In the afternoon, Lieutenant Reynolds, with Lieutenant Grigorieff as observer, bombed more barges at Dubovka, a town on the Volga forty miles north of Tsaritsin. As the fighting was now moving away from C Flight's airfield, it was decided to move the aircraft up to Tsaritsin. Captain Davies and Lieutenant Grigorieff flew to the airfield at Tsaritsin that had been nominated for use by C Flight, but looking at the field from the air they decided that it was far too small and had obstructions scattered across it, so they returned to Gniloaksaiskaya. When a White Russian squadron of Nieuports tried to land on the field, three crashed, killing one pilot.

Lieutenants Grigorieff and Webb were sent to Tsaritsin by train in an attempt to find a suitable landing ground. When they arrived back on 6 July, they confirmed that no landing ground could be found close to the rail line in Tsaritsin. The nearest one was alongside the railway station at Beketovka, a small town just five miles south of Tsaritsin and also on the Volga. (During the Second World War, when the German Army at Stalingrad surrendered they were marched through the snow to an enormous prisoner of war camp at Beketovka, many dying before they reached there.) The area for the train was in a siding next to a timber yard and a large open grassy area could be used as the airfield. Four aircraft took off to move forward to Beketovka, but one flown by Lieutenant Reynolds made a forced landing soon after take-off. After being provided with an engine, the C Flight train finally joined the DH9s at Beketovka at 19.00 hours. The other aircraft was brought in the next day.

C Flight officers and men, photographed at Beketovka.

For the next four days, no requests were made for operations by the White Army headquarters and the time was spent overhauling the machines. On 11 July, four DH9s set off to bomb Kamychin, which is 110 miles north of Tsaritsin on the Volga. One of the machines was forced to turn back with engine trouble, but the others managed to set two barges on fire. As the fighting was moving further north, Captain Davies requested that C Flight be provided with barges to enable them to operate further up the Volga, but none were available. The rail line did not run along the Volga, but north of Tsaritsin ran to the north-west.

Also on 11 July, Major Collishaw moved up from Novorossisk to the squadron headquarters at Ekaterinodar, bringing with him seven officers and 179 other ranks. Work had been going on to get the aircraft and train ready for another flight to take part in the fighting, in addition to keeping C Flight up to strength. After many difficulties and delays, the B Flight train left for the Kharkov front under the command of Captain Frogley. On 19 July, Collishaw was ordered to recall B Flight to Ekaterinodar and to send the flight to the Volga front. Practically all the members of the original C Flight had applied to be sent home, and B Flight was required to replace them.

At Beketovka, Lieutenant Grigorieff flew a DH9 solo for the first time on 13 July. Kamychin was bombed by two machines on 15 July and again on the following day, barges on the river being the main targets. Several days flying were lost during the month of July because of bad weather. It had been decided that B Flight would replace C Flight at Beketovka and would be renamed the 'new' C Flight. Two aircraft, flown by Lieutenants Verity and Clavey from the 'old' C Flight, returned to Ekaterinodar on 19 July, though Clavey had to make a forced landing fifteen miles short of the airfield. A third machine flew back on 23 July. The new C Flight train left for the Volga front on 21 July, still commanded by Captain Frogley. The first operation flown by the new C Flight took place on 25 July, when Captain Frogley and Lieutenant Cronin bombed barges and troops at Tcherni-Yar. This is a town on the Volga, ninety miles south-east of Tsaritsin. Baron Wrangel's White Armies had captured Tsaritsin, but the Red forces still controlled the river north and south of the city.

The Volga is one of the great rivers of the world. It drains most of central Russia and the western slopes of the Ural Mountains before flowing into the Caspian Sea. Running across the flat land around Tsaritsin, the river is over a mile wide. It has been one of Russia's main transport routes for centuries. In the 11th century, Vikings from Norway travelled down the Volga to serve in the Army of the Byzantine Emperor. The river flows into the Caspian Sea at the port of Astrakhan, which remained in the hands of the Bolsheviks, even though they were under attack by General Erdel's

A boat on the River Volga at Tsaritsin.

White forces. Controlling the river above and below Tsaritsin allowed the Red forces to gather gunboats from as far away as the Baltic (making their way through canals onto the Volga) and the Caspian to support their forces. River barges provided an easy form of transport for the Red Army across the featureless steppes, where there were few good roads and fewer rail lines.

A second raid was mounted on 25 July by two machines, flown by Captain Elliot and Lieutenant Hatchett. Kamychin, north of Tsaritsin, was the target for this raid and two 112 lb bombs as well as ten 20 lb bombs were dropped on a jetty and barges on the river. During the raid, a Red air force fighter attacked the DH9 crewed by Lieutenant Hatchett and his gunner Lieutenant Simmons:

> While bombing the target the above Newport [sic] appeared on our left, it made several attempts to get on our tail, where-up-on we manoeuvred for a favourable position, after firing fifty rounds from the back gun the Newport was seen to heel over and go into a steep wide circle just missing a ravine and landing on bad ground it was difficult to see if the machine crashed. A subsequent reconnaissance by Captain W. Elliot D F C and Lt. H S Laidlaw confirmed the fact that the machine had crashed in the vicinity of KAMYCHIN.[6]

This was the first enemy aircraft shot down by 47 Squadron in south Russia.

In the centre, Captains Frogley and Elliot (with Lieutenants Simmons and Hatchett).

Kamychin was bombed again on 26 July, with three hits on barges. Captain Anderson flew up from Ekaterinodar to Beketovka on 27 July, a flight of nearly 400 miles. The DH9s that were being used by the flight were not new aircraft and had already seen service during the First World War in the eastern Mediterranean. When Anderson arrived, the Red forces still controlled the River Volga north and south of Tsaritsin. The gunboats on the river were a major threat to the city. These gunboats, some of them carrying artillery as large as nine-inch, were being used to attack the White forces in Tsaritsin.

The bulk of Wrangel's Army was made up of Cossack cavalry from the north Caucasus. Most of the Red Army opposing them was also made up of cavalry. The majority of Wrangel's artillery was mounted on armoured trains and he had no way of opposing the Bolshevik gunboats on the river, apart from the aircraft of C Flight. Although he had flown for four hours in the morning, Anderson took part in his first combat mission in Russia during the afternoon of his arrival. This was an attack on Kamychin, north of Tsaritsin, by four DH9s. The target was docks and barges on the river, as well as troops on the riverbank. Three 112 lb bombs and twenty-four 20 lb bombs were dropped and 1,350 rounds of ammunition fired. The squadron diary for that day notes Anderson's role in the action:

Captain Anderson went down to 300ft to fire into barges and his machine was hit several times by machine gun fire.[7]

The raid had taken place between 16.00 hours and 19.20 hours. During the summer, that part of Russia is extremely hot and flying during the middle of the day is difficult because of air turbulence. Consequently, most the flying took place early in the morning or late in the afternoon.

On 28 July, Captain Frogley flew back to Ekaterinodar and together with Major Collishaw had a meeting with Colonel Maund regarding moving C Flight closer to the fighting, which the Russians had failed to do. On 29 July, Captain Frogley flew back to C Flight at Beketovka. The following day he had an interview with General Wrangel, but nothing seems to have come of this.

Later in the day, Frogley led a flight of three DH9s on a bombing trip to Tcherni-Yar. The pilots of the other DH9s were Captain Walter Anderson, with Lieutenant Mitchell as his observer, and Captain William Elliot, with Lieutenant Laidlaw as observer. After bombing and strafing the river traffic, Captain Anderson flew low over the target to allow Lieutenant Mitchell to take photographs, which had been requested by the Russian Army Intelligence. The DH9 was hit in the fuel tank by heavy machine-gun fire from the ground. This forced Lieutenant Mitchell to climb out on the wing to stop the flow of petrol with his thumb, clinging onto the strut between

DH9As with Liberty engines, pictured at Beketovka.

the wings with one hand as he blocked the leak with the other. As Captain Anderson turned for home, he saw that Captain Elliot's aircraft had also been hit and was gliding down with the engine stopped. Captain Anderson landed within a quarter of a mile of the other aircraft. As the DH9 touched down, several squadrons of Red cavalry began to gallop towards it. After setting their aircraft on fire, Captain Elliot and Lieutenant Laidlaw ran across to Anderson's aircraft. Mitchell had climbed back into his cockpit and opened fire on the approaching cavalry with the Lewis gun. Elliot and Laidlaw both squeezed into the observer's cockpit after Mitchell again climbed onto the wing. Anderson managed to taxi the overladen aircraft across the steppe and lift off. The rescue had taken place five miles behind enemy lines.

In a report describing the rescue, Captain Elliot wrote:

At about 4 pm on July 30th whilst escorting Capt Anderson on special operations in the vicinity of Tcherni-Yar I followed Capt. Anderson down to within 1000 feet to take oblique photographs for Russian Caucasian Army Intelligence. We were subjected to continuous heavy machine gun fire and my machine was disabled through being struck on the Starboard side of the engine through the water jacket and just above the carburettor. I was finally forced to descend about five miles behind the enemy lines in the neighbourhood of several bodies of enemy cavalry. On landing I at once set fire to my machine, and had hardly done so when I found that Capt. Anderson had also landed close by. His machine was also disabled and Lieutenant Mitchell was standing on the wing stopping a bullet hole in the tank. Lieutenant Laidlaw (my observer) and I at once got into Capt. Anderson's machine and Lieutenant Laidlaw who got in first opened fire with the Lewis gun on the nearest party of cavalry. Captain Anderson took off and flew the four of us back to our airfield at Beketovka. Lieutenant Mitchell throughout the flight of fifty minutes remained on the wing. He was dressed in shorts and a drill tunic which made it the more wonderful that he was able to withstand the hot exhaust of the engine to which, in addition to the pressure of air he was being subjected.[8]

The heat from the engine exhaust had burnt Mitchell as he struggled to hold on against the 100mph slipstream. But this cannot have been too bad, as he flew the day after. As he also became covered in petrol, any spark from the exhaust would have transformed him into a human torch.

There had been reports that the Bolsheviks would crucify any captured British pilots. But none of 47's aircrew were ever captured. Marion Aten, in his book, claimed that the British pilots carried morphine as a suicide

The DH9, flown by Captain Elliot, that crashed on 30 July 1919. Elliot claimed to have burned the aircraft but there is no sign of a fire having taken place, although it is certainly wrecked. The photograph was taken after the area was recaptured.

pill for use if they were captured, but this sounds unlikely. In reality, all British prisoners of war captured during the intervention, on all fronts, were returned in 1920, after being relatively well treated.

Colonel Maund, the senior RAF officer in south Russia, asked that Anderson and Mitchell be awarded the Victoria Cross, but in the end the pair were awarded the Distinguished Service Order (DSO) for the rescue. Major-General Sir Hugh Trenchard, the commanding officer of the RAF, wrote a memo on the type of medal the pair should receive:

> An award of the DSO to both officers would be adequate recognition. In all the 'side show' operations Cameroons, East Africa, Egypt, India, Mesopotamia the commanders of forces made it a number one point to get a Victoria Cross bestowed on somebody – it tended to lift their doings up to the sanguinary status required by the press. France had all the glory all the time.[9]

This reveals Trenchard's opinion on the importance of the forces he had sent to south Russia.

Early in the month, General Wrangel had awarded the Russian George Cross Fourth Class to the five pilots and five observers of the original C flight for 'Carrying out under hostile artillery fire air reconnaissance of the enemy positions and bombing which had valuable and important consequences for the army'. Ira Jones, who served in north Russia during this period and had shot down forty German aircraft during the First World War, had strong views about the value of the medals awarded during the Russian Intervention:

> Medals are apparently two a penny in this war. Fellows get a Distinguished Flying Cross for shows which were considered as 'all in the days work' in France. As for Russian decorations – they are bought in the shops.[10]

It is hard to view Anderson's exploits in this way, and a genuine case could have been made for the award of the Victoria Cross.

On 31 July, six sorties were carried out against transport targets. During the month of July, 47 Squadron had flown 139 hours and 5 minutes on operations and 11 hours and 55 minutes on air tests. The squadron had also dropped 4,736 lbs of bombs and fired 8,450 rounds of machine-gun ammunition.

The Training Mission during July was slowly getting itself organised. The Russians still had considerable difficulties with the RE8, and they clearly would have liked the British to have supplied them with a more modern machine. On 26 July, Major John Oliver Archer arrived in Ekaterinodar to command the Training Mission. Archer had commanded a training school in Egypt and had soon organised the mission on a better footing. He also received the necessary qualified RE8 instructors. Major Paine was transferred out of the country.

Large numbers of aircraft had been transferred to the Russian air force, and a Russian squadron was based alongside 47 Squadron at Beketovka. Captain Anderson was less than impressed with the quality of the Russian pilots:

> Their pilots were decidedly inferior; with very few exceptions they seemed to lack all flying sense, and were very much inclined to get swollen heads. After one successful solo on type, they did not bother to carry out any further practice. Consequently when they were required to fly again at a later period, this second solo would frequently prove to be their last.[11]

Lieutenant Ritchie, who taught the Russians, had a different view:

> The officers were easily taught and on the whole made good pilots, but they were very lazy and were too strict in observation of religious holidays, of which there appeared to be a great number.[12]

DH9 belonging to a Russian Squadron. Note the train in the background.

Later in July, the main tank school was moved from Ekaterinodar to
Tagenrog on the Sea of Azov. The school was established in the Baltic Works,
an armaments factory in Tagenrog, and a battle practice ground for the tanks
was set up fourteen miles outside the town. More tanks were delivered to the
Russians, making a total of sixty-seven Mk Vs and seventeen Whippets. The
tanks played a large part in the White Army advances during the summer.

The headquarters for the British Military Mission and the RAF
headquarters also began the move to Tagenrog late in July.

NOTES

[1] National Archives, 62 Wing diary
[2] Ibid.
[3] Ibid.
[4] Ibid.
[5] Bilney, C. N. H., unpublished memoir
[6] National Archives, Hatchett, combat report
[7] National Archives, 47 Squadron diary
[8] National Archives, Elliot W., report
[9] National Archives, Trenchard, H., report
[10] Jones, Ira, *An Air Fighter's Scrapbook*, Vintage Aviation Library,
    London, 1990, page 130
[11] National Archives, Anderson, W. F., War Experiences
[12] National Archives, Ritchie, A. P., War Experiences

Detail of picture on p. 75

CHAPTER TWELVE

AUGUST 1919

By the start of August, the Armed Forces of South Russia seemed to be victorious everywhere. On the western flank, after taking Kharkov, the Volunteer Army was marking time to recover from the last advance, but at the end of August it moved forward to capture Kiev. In the centre of the front, the Don Army was preparing for a major raid by the Don cavalry leader Mamontov and 10,000 Cossacks. On 10 August, this force broke through the Red Army lines and by 18 August it entered the town of Tambov, 125 miles behind the front line. Mamontov then turned west and continue to operate behind the lines until the end of August. But, in reality, this raid degenerated into looting and plunder by the Cossacks. General Sidorin, the Don Cossack leader, was only able to keep in touch with Mamontov by using aircraft to carry messages.

General Wrangel had been ordered by General Denikin to continue his advance north along the Volga. After capturing Kamyshin, the next major town was Saratov. By now, Wrangel's Caucasian Army was only a shadow of its former self. With most of the heavy units gone, the Army was made up mostly of Kuban Cossack cavalry units. Some of the regiments were now down to a few hundred men. Both the horses and the troops were exhausted. General Denikin either could not or would not provide any replacements.

The Kuban Cossack parliament had disagreed with General Denikin on political matters and would not provide more men or horses for Wrangel. The Caucasian Army managed to reach Saratov but failed to capture it.

The Red Army facing General Denikin's forces grew to 170,000 during the late summer. With the defeat of Admiral Kolchak's forces on the eastern front, more troops were released for the southern front. The Armed Forces of South Russia were conscripting recruits from the territory they had captured. But the replacements were never of the same quality as the original volunteer forces. Even with conscription, Denikin could never match the numbers of the Red Army.

In Moscow, a major disagreement over the way to counter-attack against General Denikin developed during August. The Red Army leader Kamanov decided that the main thrust should be against the eastern end of the line and General Wrangel's Caucasian Army. The attack was to be along a south-west axis towards Rostov and be carried out by the 9th and 10th Armies under General Shorin. In later years, both Stalin and Trotsky claimed that they opposed this strategy. On 15 August, this major attack drove the Caucasus Army back to Kamyshin. Wrangel had no choice but to retreat in order to hold his much reduced forces together. On 14 August, General Wrangel had visited the Kuban parliament in Ekaterinodar to plead for more reinforcements. The Red 10th Army continued their attack and on 22 August Kamyshin also fell. By 28 August, Dubovka, which was only forty miles north of Tsaritsin, had been captured.

On the Caspian, the two machines from 221 Squadron that had been attached to General Dratzenka's forces carried out four sorties on 1 August. These were reconnaissance flights over the mouth of the Volga and the coastline south of Astrakhan. The two machines returned to Petrovsk on 2 August. A raid on Astrakhan was attempted by three DH9As on 3 August, but the aircraft turned back because of thick mist. Bad weather also forced the return of a bombing raid to Lagan on 6 August. One of the bombing force was Lieutenant Lynch, who recorded the abortive attack in his log-book:

DH9As at Petrovsk airfield being prepared for a raid on Astrakhan.

6/8/19 06.40hrs. DH9A 807, Observer Lt. Ham, Time in Air 2Hrs. and 50mins, Height 11.000Ft. Course Petrovsk – Astrakhan – Petrovsk, Engine very hot. Forced to return owing to thick fog NE Bermach. Radiator burst just before landing.[1]

It had been arranged that 62 Wing would leave the Caspian area by the end of the month. The bad feeling against the British in this area was increasing and many of the men were suffering from fever. Lieutenant O. R. Gayford wrote:

At the beginning of August I was invalided home with malaria and complication.[2]

Colonel Bowhill, writing in the Wing diary, reflected upon the decision to go:

The fever is still very bad and it is only with great difficulty that I have been able to carry out any raids at all. My doctors state it is imperative that the officers and men now at 221 Squadron should leave the country. On account of this, and having received your authority, the wing leaves Petrovsk on the 18th August 1919.[3]

The redoubtable D. B. Knock wrote in his diary of his hopes of leaving Russia:

1/8/19 ... growing unrest in all ranks about going home, but am notified by adjutant that I am on a draft for England![4]

Knock went home by the southern route, by sea to Baku and across the Caucasus by rail to Batum. The train he was travelling in was derailed when the points were sabotaged; the driver was killed and the train wrecked. A fresh locomotive was found but at another point on the track the train was again attacked, this time by showers of stones. Knock was relieved when the train reached Batum and he could see the British warships in the harbour.

On 10 August, a raid was mounted on Lagan and three big barges were bombed. Because of mist, the results of the bombing could not be seen. On the flight back to Petrovsk, the aircraft had a 55 mph head wind. One aircraft was forced to land through engine failure on the way to the target, as reported by its pilot, Lieutenant Lynch:

10/8/19 06.30Hrs. DH9A 807, Observer G. R. Thompson, Time in Air 40Mins. Height 4,000Ft. Course Petrovsk – Astrakhan – Petrovsk,

HMS *Orlionoch* alongside the jetty at Petrovsk port, with Short 184 number N9078 being hoisted on board.

Engine very hot but running well on taking off. Radiator burst SW 10 miles of Chechen. Engine seized up. Was forced to land on Uck Peninsula SW of Chechen and abandoned Machine.[5]

Luckily, this was behind Volunteer Army lines. On 11 August, two DH9As left Petrovsk and dropped food to Lynch and Ham, the crew of the aircraft that had force-landed. The last raid by 221 Squadron was on 12 August. At Mogilny, bombs were dropped on shipping and wharfs. One machine landed at Beryuzak to report the results to General Dratzenka.

During August, Captain Bilney and his men returned from Guryev. The rest of the month was spent handing over the remaining 266 Squadron aircraft and stores to the local White Russian forces. Captain Sadler was at sea for most of the month on board the *Orlionoch*, with two of the Short 184s, but on 26 August the *Orlionoch* and the aircraft were handed over to the Volunteer Navy, along with the rest of the British ships on the Caspian. On 27 August, Sadler and the remaining Squadron personnel left Petrovsk.

Captain Bilney left Petrovsk by the northern route, by rail north of the Caucasus Mountains to Ekaterinodar and Novorossisk. He wrote the following description of the trip:

We left Petrovsk the way we had come, in cattle trucks, but the weather was warmer and, we had a great send off, the piece de resistance being the sight of our beloved Wing Commander being embraced and kissed on both cheeks by the local Russian General. Ginger Bowhill was the last man in the world to enjoy anything of this sort. Our journey took us across the Northern Caucasus and I have vivid memories of traversing miles of country devoted entirely to growing sunflowers, maize and unlimited supplies of luscious water melons.[6]

Lieutenant L. H. Kemp also left by the northern route:

...We were told we were to leave all our stores and aircraft and we left by train and the unfortunate situation was that we were compelled to go through villages that we had been bombing and you can imagine the reception at times was a little hostile.[7]

Kemp's train was fired on during the journey and a bullet lodged in an almanac he had in his luggage.

221 Squadron had handed over the remainder of the DH9 aircraft to the local Russians, but the DH9As were earmarked for 47 Squadron and most of these were transported by rail and sea, by the *Ark Royal*,

to Novorossisk. Most of the 221 pilots chose to go home, but a number volunteered to serve with 47 Squadron and the Training Mission.

Early in the month of August, the White Army under General Wrangel carried out an attack on Tcherni-Yar and most of C Flight's efforts were directed in support of this attack. On 1 August, three sorties were mounted against the railway station in Tcherni-Yar. Captain Frogley and Captain Palmer flew two bombing raids against barges on the following day. In order to reduce the distance between the airfield at Beketovka and the fighting at Tcherni-Yar, a forward landing ground was established at Viasovka, south-east of Tsaritsin. Motor transport was sent forward from Beketovka to support the aircraft landing at Viasovka. No operations were flown on 3 August, but on 4 August Captain Frogley and Lieutenant Harding had an interview with General Wrangel, during which he explained to them his plans for the forthcoming attack.

The Caucasian Army launched the attack on 5 August. Three DH9s flown by Captain Anderson and Lieutenants Cronin and Hatchett were used to support this attack. Shipping on the river was bombed and the three aircraft landed at Viasovka before flying back to Beketovka. In the afternoon, Captain Frogley led a further raid, accompanied by Captain Elliot flying another DH9. Enemy-held trenches were attacked with machine-gun fire and barges on the river were bombed. At 17.20 hours, a third raid by three aircraft was mounted, and shipping on the river was again bombed and trenches machine-gunned. During the day, sixty-seven bombs had been dropped and 2,300 rounds of machine-gun ammunition fired in sixteen hours of flying time.

The Red Army continued to hold the River Volga north and south of Tsaritsin and carried on building up its river fleets in order to dominate the river, as Wrangel had very few boats available to him. The boats were also used as mobile artillery batteries to support the fighting on the riverbanks. Captain Anderson described the fleets:

> Their two large fleets consisted of about fifty craft each. These fleets were composed of rather a miscellaneous assortment ranging from small tugs with I think, a three pounder gun, to large barges with 9.2 inch guns. They were mostly ordinary riverboats with guns mounted on them, but they had a certain number of armoured river gunboats. There appeared to be little attempt at co-ordination between these two fleets as they never seemed to make any serious attempt to attack simultaneously; this of course allowed General Wrangel to make full use of his advantage of interior lines.[8]

The aircraft of 47 Squadron, and the White air force unit stationed at Beketovka, were the only means available to General Wrangel of countering the gunboat fleets.

The Army continued to attack Tcherni-Yar on 6 August, and during the day C Flight carried out ten sorties against enemy troops and transport in the town, as well as shipping on the river. Lieutenant Mitchell was wounded in the foot by machine-gun fire from the ground. The ground attack by the Caucasian Army continued for some time but was not successful in taking the town. No operational flying by C Flight was carried out for the next few days.

On 8 August, thirteen DH9As arrived at Novorossisk on board the *Ark Royal*. The aircraft, which had been used by 221 Squadron, had been delivered by sea from Batum. It was intended that A Flight would be equipped with the DH9As, and considerable effort was put into getting the aircraft serviceable. But many spares were missing or had been stolen after they had arrived in Russia.

In the early hours of 15 August, Captain R. E. Eversden was shot dead at Ekaterinodar by a sentry guarding the squadron train. Captain Eversden, for some reason never made clear, had climbed under the train. The sentry, who had been fired on three times during the night, challenged Captain Eversden and when he received no answer shot him dead. The sentry was exonerated at an enquiry. Captain Eversden's mother never received any explanation of his death or received his personal effects. She was reduced to writing to General Allenby, the commanding officer in the Middle East, before she received any satisfaction.

On 16 August, at Beketovka , after several days of no operational flying, Captains Anderson and Elliot again took off to bomb Tcherni-Yar from 2,000 ft. On the morning of 17 August, three aircraft bombed transport and troop targets in Staritskoe, 15 miles north of Tcherni-Yar; two more sorties were undertaken in the afternoon. Two DH9s, flown by Captain Frogley and Lieutenant Cronin, again bombed Staritskoe on 18 August. In the afternoon, Captains Elliot and Anderson bombed Prist-Eltonskaya on the east side of the Volga, as recorded in the squadron diary:

Height 1,500 feet. Four 112lb. and sixteen 20lb. Bombs were dropped onto troops and horse transport in the square and streets of the town. Severe damage was caused. Troops and animals appeared panic stricken. Hits were also obtained on trains in the station and on bridge close to the station. 900 rounds S. A. A. were fired amongst the troops causing many casualties.[9]

The next day, Lieutenants Hatchett and Day bombed barges and gunboats on the Volga between Tcherni-Yar and Staritskoe. They followed this up by firing 900 rounds at the personnel on the barges.

Lieutenant M. H. Aten reported for duty at Ekaterinodar on 19 August. Lieutenant Aten was an American, born at Amarillo in Texas in 1894 but brought up in California. His father had been a famous Texas Ranger. He had joined the RAF but had been too late to take part in the First World War. Many years later, he was to write a very fanciful account of 47 Squadron called *Last Train Over Rostov Bridge*. In this, he claimed to be the first person in the squadron to have shot down a Red air force 'plane and that altogether he shot down five Russian aircraft. One of these, he claimed, was the leading Red fighter ace, who had shot down twelve White aircraft. Lieutenant Aten did fly with B Flight when it reached the front and he was awarded a DFC for his work in Russia, but no record can be found for any of his combat claims. He claimed to have shot down aircraft in April 1919, when he was not even in Russia and 47 Squadron had not entered combat. His book should only be viewed as semi-fictional.

During the afternoon of 19 August, the workshop lorry and engine repair shop at Ekaterinodar caught fire and were burned out, destroying engine spares and tools. The local Russian fire brigade helped to put the fire out. On 20 August, three aircraft from Beketovka raided Staritskoe and Tcherni-Yar, dropping bombs on trenches and shipping on the river. A Red fighter attacked Lieutenant Cronin, as he stated in his combat report:

> 0810 hours over Tcherni-Yar an enemy Nieuport was seen to dive on me on right rear. My front gun was not working, I circled round to give my observer (Lieut. Mercer) a field of fire. After 10 minutes fighting during which 4 bursts of fire were exchanged from about 50 to 100 yards the enemy was seen to go down in control after a burst of fire into his left wing, out of which splinters flew. He was observed to go down over the marshes N. E. of Tcherni-Yar and was then lost sight of. He was undoubtedly badly shot up.[10]

On 21 August, seven officers and eighty-five other ranks who had not volunteered for service in Russia left Ekaterinodar for Constantinople. Captain J. W. B. Grigson, Captain B. G. H. Keymer, Lieutenant M. J. Langley, Lieutenant E. M. Gradden, and Lieutenant H. W. L. Buckley from 221 Squadron had volunteered to serve with 47 Squadron and were taken on the strength. Lieutenant Vic Clow joined the Training Mission at Taganrog as an instructor.

Also on 21 August, two DH9s left Ekaterinodar for Beketovka, but both of them made forced landings on the way, requiring mechanics to

be flown out to them. On 25 August, two aircraft from C Flight bombed
barges and trenches at Staritskoe and Tcherni-Yar. The Red air force had
an air base at Tcherni-Yar, and this was also bombed. As they circled the
airfield, Lieutenant Hatchett, with Lieutenant Simmons as his gunner, saw
an enemy Nieuport with a red nose, a red disc on the rudder, and black
crosses on the fuselage, taking off. Their combat report described what
happened:

> The Nieuport was seen taking off. We waited our time for him to gain
> height. The hostile machine climbed to 500 feet above us and then dived.
> 50 rounds were fired from the back gun striking hostile in fuselage but
> doing no damage. The back gun then jammed and we broke off the
> fight.[11]

The fact that Hatchett waited for the fighter to take off and climb to attack
his aircraft (he was at 4,000 ft) shows his confidence in himself, his gunner,
and his aircraft.

Captain Anderson bombed the Red airfield on 26 August, destroying
one hangar and burning two Nieuports. Anderson and Captain Frogley
also bombed a barge on the river on 27 August. The barge, with two
observation balloons attached, was sunk. Three Distinguished Flying
Crosses were awarded to members of 47 Squadron for work done on
27 August. These were for Lieutenant H. E. Simmons, Lieutenant J. R.
Hatchett, and Lieutenant N. Greenslade. The citation for Lieutenant
Simmons reads:

> On the 27/8/19 at Tcherni Yar, Lt. Simmons flying a DH9 carried out
> work usually assigned to scouts, descending to water level and attacking
> a large fleet in spite of concentrated fire from anti-aircraft guns on
> almost all the vessels, from field guns, machine guns, and rifles from
> the river banks. This daring attack created great confusion amongst the
> Bolsheviks, who suffered heavy casualties. He has in addition carried
> out many raids into the enemy country, and has shown on all occasions
> a disregard for danger and devotion to duty which has earned him the
> admiration of our allies.[12]

The other two officers also received their awards for the same attack on
the Russian riverboats.

Also on 27 August, Captain Elliot, who had been rescued by Anderson,
was carrying Major W. N. Williamson, an Army officer, as a passenger.
They were trying to find an arms dump where the Russians had stored gas
shells given to them by the British. When Captain Elliot tried to restart

the engine of his DH9, he was struck on the left arm by the propeller and severely injured. Major Williamson carried Elliot to the nearest hospital. A future air chief marshal was carried down a road in the middle of Russia by a future general and a Russian woman. Elliot recovered and was returned to Britain.

Lieutenant Cronin, with Lieutenant Mercer as his observer, attacked an armoured car on 28 August, killing the driver and overturning the car in a ditch. During another bombing raid on the same day, C Flight had their first combat casualty. Captain Anderson, with Captain McLennon as his observer, had attacked an observation balloon attached to one of the riverboats, which had been directing the gunfire from the boats on the river. The attack was carried out at low level using incendiary bullets; the balloon was set on fire and the crew killed. The balloon had belonged to the 7th Airlift Detachment. During the attack, Captain McLennon was hit by ground fire and was found to be dead when Anderson landed back at Beketovka. Anderson described the incident:

> They re-took Kamyshin and were rapidly advancing down the river. The success of this advance was due principally to them having obtained some kite balloons for use in directing their gunfire. In my first raid against this advancing fleet I had the great misfortune to lose my observer, Captain McLennon who was shot through the artery in his left leg while we were in the act of bombing one of their balloons; he of course bled to death in a very few minutes.[13]

General Wrangel awarded the St George's Cross to both Anderson and McLennon. The citation reads:

> Captain Anderson pilot and Captain McLennon observer of the 47th Squadron, notwithstanding the difficulty of observation in consequence of strong enemy fire, performed their task with the utmost disregard for their own safety, and giving valuable information concerning the enemy and destroying an enemy captive balloon, in attacking which they were forced to descend into fierce rifle fire. During the performance of this attack, observer Captain McLennon was Killed.[14]

During the same air attack, the gunboat *Vigilant* was hit by a bomb that killed six of the crew and injured fourteen others.

In the course of the month of August, the squadron had dropped 17,428 lbs of bombs and fired 19,740 rounds of ammunition on operations. This had involved 241 hours and 5 minutes of operational flying and 3 hours and 20 minutes of test flying.

In early August, 28 other ranks with the tank school refused to continue serving in south Russia and had to be sent home. None of these men had volunteered in the first place and must have wondered what they were doing in the middle of Russia when the war that they had volunteered for was over. On 16 August, Major Sayer arrived in south Russia as a representative of the War Office to inspect the work of the tanks in Russia. Major Sayer described the conditions at the tank school at Taganrog:

> The personnel of our Tank Detachment in Tagenrog are very comfortably quartered and cared for. To all intents and purposes there is no work to be done in the afternoons, and there is both time and facilities for sport and amusements ... There is also plenty of swimming, boxing and boating to keep our fellows fit and happy ... For the delectation of the troops in the evenings there is a very excellent gardens, where plays a band and where may be found most of the youth and beauty of the neighbourhood. There are several cinemas also in Taganrog, and greatest joy of all, a theatre in which Denikin's own string orchestra plays two or three times a week.[15]

The RAF Training Mission, the British Military Mission, and the RAF HQ had also moved to Taganrog. This seemingly idyllic existence at Taganrog, however, was not to last much longer.

NOTES

[1]　National Archives, Lynch, John Brayne, log-book
[2]　National Archives, Gayford, O. R., War Experiences
[3]　National Archives, 62 Wing diary
[4]　Knock, D. B., 'An Armourer's Diary', *Popular Flying*, May 1938
[5]　National Archives, Lynch, John Brayne, log-book
[6]　Bilney, C. N. H., unpublished memoir
[7]　Kemp, L. H., unpublished memoir
[8]　National Archives, Anderson, W. F., War Experiences
[9]　National Archives, 47 Squadron diary
[10]　National Archives, Cronin, combat report
[11]　National Archives, Hatchett, combat report
[12]　National Archives, Simmons, medal citation
[13]　National Archives, Anderson, W. F., War Experiences
[14]　National Archives, Anderson, W. F., medal citation
[15]　Sayers, Major, 'A Visit to the South Russian Tank Corps', *The Tank Corps Journal*, December 1919

Detail of picture on p. 209.

CHAPTER THIRTEEN

SEPTEMBER 1919

During September, the Armed Forces of South Russia met with mixed fortunes. On the western front, General Mai-Maevsky continued the advance of the Volunteer Army. The western front of the Army was the nearest to Moscow, and Mai-Maevsky seemed to be heading directly for the capital city. Volunteer Army armoured trains steamed into Kursk on 20 September. Kursk is on the direct rail line to Moscow and only 250 miles south of the city.

The Don Cossack forces under Sidorin continued to press forward, and the Cossack raid behind Red Army lines commanded by General Mamontov continued. Kozlov was captured and Voronezh held for a short period. Trotsky was at Kozlov, which was headquarters of the Red Army Southern Front, and he was forced to flee for his life in his special train. In the middle of the month, the raiding force broke back through the Red Army lines. They brought with them enormous amounts of plunder carried in ox carts. Many of the Cossacks now chose to go home with their loot. The results of the Mamontov raid were mixed at best. Trotsky was forced to admit that the Red Army did not have enough cavalry, and after this large cavalry units were formed under the command of General Dumenko and General Budenny. It was after seeing the effects of the Mamontov raid that Trotsky framed his famous statement 'Proletarians to horse'. Later in the month, Trotsky was moved to Petrograd and Stalin was sent to the southern front as a commissar, not a direct military leader.

On the Volga front, Wrangel was facing the major Red Army attack against the Armed Forces of South Russia. This was intended to break through to the Black Sea. The Red Army had driven the Caucasian Army back to Tsaritsin by the beginning of September. For a short period, it looked like the city would fall but Wrangel managed to stop the advance and drove the Red Army a short distance back up the Volga. This was a major victory for the Caucasian Army, as they had been reduced in size and were worn out with constant fighting. The Red forces had outnumbered them by a considerable margin; General Wrangel and his troops had performed outstandingly well.

By early September, the Red Army had recaptured Dubovka, only forty miles north of Tsaritsin, and established an airfield and seaplane base on the river. Captain Frogley, commanding C Flight, had complained that C Flight had been too far away from the fighting and had asked to be moved closer, but in fact the fighting had moved back to C Flight. On 1 September, after taking off at 05.30 hours, Captain Frogley and Captain Anderson carried out a raid on Dubovka. Shipping on the river was bombed and machine-gunned. In the afternoon, two other sorties were flown against Dubovka. The following day, only one sortie was flown, by Captain Frogley, and bombs were dropped on troops in the village at Dubovka. It began to look like the Red forces might retake Tsaritsin, and C Flight moved airfield on 5 September to the village of Gniloaksaiskaya, seventy miles south-east of Beketovka. Captain Palmer crashed one of the DH9s (C6337) while landing. Between two and four sorties were flown each day against the riverboats or the railway station at Achtuba on the east bank of the Volga.

On 7 September, Lieutenant Mercer wrote in his log-book:

7/9/19 Time in Air 2Hrs. and 30Mins. Aircraft DH9 D3149, Pilot Lt. Cronin. Destination Boats North of Tsaritsin, Nature of Flight Bombing Raid, Remarks Two enemy machines seen. They ran away.[1]

General Wrangel had been away from the front and returned during the first week of September; an improvement in the position of the Caucasian Army followed on from this. Wrangel ordered the evacuation of the entire city:

I ordered the evacuation of the town to begin. Seven trains were to leave every day. The first thing to be hurried off was the war material; then the civil and military administrations were to go; lastly those civilians who wanted to leave the town ... There was luggage room for each person to take one trunk and no more ... On the first day only four of the seven trains got away, and on the second day only three ... I singled out several Cossacks from my escort and went to the station. A passenger train was just leaving. The carriages were full of pianos, mirrors and valuable furniture. I had it all thrown out and smashed. Then I discovered a train with locked carriages. The documents said that they were loaded with munitions. I had them opened. They were not full of munitions but of

passengers, who wanted to get away and to take their merchandise with
them. They informed me that they had bribed the station master and
two of his colleagues. I had these three employees court-marshalled and
they were hanged the same day ... Eight trains left daily instead of only
seven.[2]

The station master and one of his colleagues were hanged at the station
and another in the town square. The body of the station master was hung
over the entrance to the station at Tsaritsin and anybody entering had to
duck underneath his legs. Wrangel was ruthless but effective.

Wrangel finally received reinforcements on 2 September. These included
one infantry brigade and one fresh cavalry division. The full weight of the
Red 10th and 11th Armies was directed against the Caucasian Army on
3 September. Wrangel kept his infantry in Tsaritsin and kept his cavalry
on the flank. The Red forces, including crack Red Navy marines, broke
through but were finally driven back by Wrangel personally leading a
cavalry charge of his own escort troops. Captain Bulgakov, one of the
soldiers in the Caucasian Army, described the event:

I glanced to the right and saw two horsemen coming up at a trot: It was
General Wrangel and his fanion bearer. The General trotted past me; I
saw him draw his sword. A minute later he was charging at the head
of his escort squadron. They burst into the Red ranks, sabering. Those
sailors who could not get out of the way blew themselves up with hand
grenades.[3]

Wrangel stopped the Red attack on the city and then sent his cavalry
round behind the Red forces, cutting them off. In a three-day battle, the
Caucasian Army captured 18,000 prisoners and 31 guns.

On 14 September, Major Collishaw flew up to C Flight from Ekaterinodar
to take control of the squadron's operations, and over the next few weeks
led many of the squadron's bombing raids. The following day, Captain
Anderson and Lieutenant Hatchett carried out a raid, flying two DH9s,
on troop barges on the Volga. An artillery observation balloon attached to
the beach and a barge used for towing the balloon were destroyed at low
level. Each of the aircraft was carrying two 112 lb bombs and eight 20 lb
bombs. While carrying out another raid on Dubovka on 16 September, the
two aircraft flown by Lieutenants Cronin and Day were attacked by a Red
air force Nieuport, as they related in their report:

While over Chirokoe we were flying north when an enemy machine
was observed four miles in rear and flying towards us. The two DH9s

The barge *Commune*, used as a mobile base for seaplanes on the River Volga at Dubovka. The *Commune* was bombed by Captain Anderson on 17 September 1919.

immediately turned to meet him. The enemy scout dived in between the tails of our machines and was met with heavy and effective cross fire from Lewis Guns, his propeller was seen to stop and he went down in a long steep dive followed by our machines, which were unable to overtake him. Enemy scout was last seen ten feet above ground over Dubovka flying south.[4]

In Soviet records, this incident is shown as occurring on 17 September, but no British pilots claim to have shot down a Russian aircraft on that date. Two Russian Nieuports had taken off from Dubovka, one piloted by Tumansky and one by Pyatevich. Tumansky had taken off without releasing the ropes tying down the Nieuport, and this had damaged the aircraft, forcing him to return to base. Pyatevich had attacked two DH9s, but the Nieuport had been hit by at least thirty rounds fired by the British aircraft. He was forced to carry out an emergency landing on sandy ground close to the Volga. Although he was not seriously injured, Pyatevich's face was severely cut by broken glass. During the afternoon of 16 September, Captain Anderson and Lieutenant Hatchett bombed more barges, an armoured car, and Red Army infantry.

At Dubovka, the Red air force had established the Volga-Caspian Naval Air Division. This unit had twelve seaplanes (M-5s, M-9s, and M-20s) and three Nieuports on its strength. Commanding officer for this force was S. E. Stolyarsky. The seaplanes were carried on a large barge, which acted as a mobile base. This barge was called the *Commune* and was towed on the river by a tug. From 4 September, the seaplanes began to bomb

Another view of the *Commune*. When the barge was bombed on 17 September, five aircraft were destroyed, two men killed, and eight men wounded.

Tsaritsin, with a number of small bombs and leaflets being dropped on the city. On 6 and 7 September, the railway station was bombed. Five raids were carried out at night. The rail line bringing supplies into Tsaritsin was also bombed.

At 13.10 hours on 17 September, Captain Anderson and Lieutenant Day, with Lieutenants Addison and Buckley, took off to attack the flying boat base at Dubovka. A Nieuport Scout was destroyed on the airfield by the bombing. The *Commune* barge, with eight flying boats on board, was hit by two 20 lb bombs, causing considerable damage. In addition, 600 rounds of machine-gun ammunition was fired at the flying boats. Russian records say that there were only seven seaplanes on the barge and that five of them were destroyed. Two bombs hit the barge, with the result that two men were killed and eight wounded. Over the next few days, bad weather prevented any further operational flying.

On 18 September, Colonel Maund received a message from the leader of the White Russian air force:

These last few days I have had the pleasure of reading in the daily reports of flying of 47 Sqdn. RAF, about the extraordinary work of the British pilots, especially Major Collishaw. I beg you to accept and transmit to Major Collishaw from the whole Russian Aviation, our sincere admiration of his brilliant activity.[5]

Major Raymond Collishaw, photographed during his time in Russia.

On 19 September, eight Sopwith Camel fighters arrived at Novorossisk. These were not new aircraft but had been used by the RNAS at Mudros in the Aegean. Captain Kinkead, who was to use the Camels operationally, proceeded from Ekaterinodar to Novorossisk with Lieutenant Grigorieff to inspect the aircraft. Four of the Camels were scrapped but work was started to make the other four airworthy. The first flight took place from Ekaterinodar on 22 September.

On 19 September, the British Military Mission received a message from the War Office:

> The bombing of Moscow is not to be allowed at present by British Air Force or No 47 Squadron, as there is no military value in this operation.[6]

There have been stories that a bombing raid on Moscow was planned, but the British forces had been specifically ordered not to do so.

A major effort was mounted on 20 September by C Flight and during the course of the day fourteen 112 lb bombs and seventy 20 lb bombs were dropped on Dubovka. One DH9 was hit by anti-aircraft fire and was forced to land; the aircraft managed to reach friendly territory but was burned out and destroyed after landing. There were no casualties. On 22 September, C Flight moved back up to Beketovka, as the situation on the ground had stabilised and the Red Army advance had been stopped. The squadron diary for 22 September reads:

> C Flight moves to Beketovka. Eleven raids on troops North of Tsaritsin. Aerial combat in which two DH9s shot down enemy Nieuport and forced it to land. Bombing had good effect, causing panic and many casualties.[7]

No further details can be found for the combat mentioned as occurring on 22 September.

On 23 September, Mercer wrote in his log-book:

> 23/9/19 Time in Air 3Hrs. Aircraft DH9 D3149, Pilot Lt. Cronin. Destination Tcherni-Yar, Nature of Flight Bombing Raid, Remarks One enemy Nieuport seen in air.[8]

Heavy raids on the gunboat fleet took place on 24, 25, 26, and 27 September. On 25 September, Lieutenant A. H. Day was wounded while attacking the riverboats. Collishaw later wrote about the bombing of riverboats:

One of our bases was only 12 miles from Stalingrad (Tsaritsin) and we operated a shuttle service, our planes landing and remaining only long enough to refuel, take on more bombs and ammunition, and then taking off again. I conceived the idea of using 230-pound anti-submarine bombs against the river vessels, and instructed my crews to try for near misses rather than direct hits. These tactics worked well, the terrific under-water blast being extremely effective against the light gunboats. We managed to sink or disable most of these Red river craft and the remainder withdrew.[9]

The American air power strategist General Billy Mitchell was also a proponent of the near miss when attacking ships. He called this the 'water hammer effect' and used it in tests to sink captured German Navy ships in the early 1920s.

The B Flight train was finally ready and left Ekaterinodar for the trip to Beketovka on 24 September. The Russian pilot Lieutenant Grigorieff was again in nominal command. The real commander of B Flight was Captain Samuel Kinkead, who had been born in South Africa. He had joined the RNAS in 1915 and had served in the Mediterranean and in France. Flying Bristol Scouts, Nieuports, and Camels he had shot down thirty-two aircraft during the First World War. Later, in the early 1920s, he again served under Major Collishaw in 30 Squadron. Kinkead was killed in 1928 off the Isle of White, when he crashed while trying to break the world airspeed record. Ira Jones, who was no mean pilot himself, wrote about Kinkead after his death:

> When Kinkead, still a Flight Lieutenant, went deep into the Solent in his Supermarine S5 (Napier engine) late in the afternoon of March 12 1928, when attempting to break the world speed record, the RAF lost without doubt, its finest junior [sic] officer. He was remarkably brave, a brilliant pilot, ideal leader and straight as a die in his dealings with his juniors and his seniors. He was modest in the extreme ... Kinkead did not receive any decorations and promotion for his magnificent peacetime work. He was junior to officers who were unworthy of cleaning his shoes. Many brave airmen had gone before Kinkead and I feel sure that Valhalla was well lit up on the night of March 12, 1928.[10]

In Iraq, during the 1920s, Kinkead carried out an exploit much the same as Anderson's, when he had landed his DH9A alongside another aircraft that had made a forced landing and rescued the crew while under fire from dissident Arabs. Sam Kinkead was the real thing.

Captain Kinkead, with Lieutenant Aten and Captain Burns-Thomson, left Ekaterinodar on 27 September, flying in three Camels, to meet B Flight's train at Beketovka. The Camels had a shorter range than the DH9s and it was

Captain Samuel Kinkead, in the cockpit of his Sopwith Camel.

intended that the three machines would spend the night at Velikoknyajeskaya airfield, half-way to Beketovka. Captain Burns-Thomson crashed his Camel on landing, wrecking his landing gear, and the aircraft had to be sent back to Ekaterinodar by train. Captain Kinkead and Lieutenant Aten arrived at Beketovka on 28 September. No bombing raids were flown that day because of high winds. Captain Rowan Heywood Daley, the fourth member of B Flight, left Ekaterinodar for Beketovka on 28 September, flying a Camel. He had shot down three German aircraft during the war while flying a Sopwith Triplane and a Camel. He was killed in an air-to-air crash in 1923.

Continuous action by 47 Squadron had forced the Red air force to move fighter aircraft from Astrakhan to Tcherni-Yar, now that 221 Squadron was no longer bombing Astrakhan. These reinforcements included the two Naval fliers D. N. Shchekin and A. P. Korotkov, who were stationed with their Nieuport Scouts on the airfield at Tcherni-Yar.

The bad weather continued on 29 September at Beketovka and the first joint mission by C and B Flights was not until 30 September. Barges on the river were again bombed both north and south of Tsaritsin. Captain Kinkead was escorting DH9s on a photographic reconnaissance mission over Tcherni-Yar when two Nieuport Scouts attacked them. Captain Kinkead, flying one of the Camels, shot one of the Nieuports down and it was seen to crash into the Volga. It was Shchekin and Korotkov who were flying the two Nieuports; Kinkead had shot down the one flown by Shchekin. Korotkov escaped by diving away. Although Shchekin's Nieuport crashed into the river, the pilot was seen to escape from the wreck, but he was unable to swim to the shore and drowned. Kinkead had repaid Shchekin for shooting down Mantle and Ingram. A month later, Korotkov crashed while flying a SPAD 7 and was killed. Also on 30 September, the first two DH9As were flown up to Beketovka.

During the month of September, 47 Squadron had flown 135 hours and 20 minutes on operations and 13 hours and 40 minutes on test flying. On operations, 11,622 lbs of bombs had been dropped and 8,150 rounds of machine-gun ammunition had been fired.

The Training Mission continued to teach the Russian pilots to fly the RE8s, but the Russians had considerable trouble with the aircraft. A number of Russians crashed while flying the RE8 and some of the aircrew were killed. The Russians spread rumours that the RE8 was a death trap and many pilots absolutely refused to fly it. It was a difficult aircraft to fly and the British had had similar difficulties when they had introduced it into service in late 1916. Nonetheless, over 3,000 RE8s were built and over 1,500 were still in service with the RAF at the end of the First World War. It was perhaps not the best choice of aircraft to have sent to Russia. A report written by the Training Mission described the Russian pilots:

> No 6 Don Squadron only 6 pilots came for instruction instead of 10. One was sent away for disobedience of orders. One went solo once, and refused to fly any more. One went solo once, crashed on his second solo and is now in hospital. One Sprained his arm when due for solo ... In the case of Lt. Ritchie's unit one evening he reported three ready for solo next day. One died, one went sick, and the other was sent away on special duty to Kharkov. Captain Head reports that in his Squadron he has no hope of two pilots out of seven pilots ever going solo on RE8s.[11]

The pilots of the Training Mission all applied to join 47 Squadron, but this was refused.

The White air force was supplied with other types of British aircraft apart from the RE8s. They operated DH9s and Camels reasonably successfully. Describing the White air force, Captain Grigson wrote:

> The state of the Flying Service was curious. Their mechanics were very good; much better than our own as tradesmen. The pilots and observers dreaded the consequences of a forced landing and capture. Their morale was distinctly low. As a result, they were not exactly pushing near the front line! They had some excuse; their machines were an odd collection of old Spads, L.V.G.'s, Nieuports and an occasional Sopwith 1½ Strutter. They were woefully short of spares, tools and materials. In fact most of their spares had to be made in their own workshops.[12]

Describing the troops that made up the Armed Forces of South Russia, Grigson continued:

> The state of the ground troops was extraordinary. I saw battalions going to the front in rags with their equipment tied up with string. Many of them were bare footed until they got boots from their prisoners. There were practically no anaesthetics or drugs. Rations were scanty – they lived on the country. Still the spirit of the Caucasian Army was excellent. They were on the Tsaritsin front, under the command of General Baron Wrangel. Wrangel was the main spring of his army. He was popular with his men – a most unusual thing for an Russian officer.[13]

By September, the British had begun to supply enormous amounts of material to south Russia, but in many cases this never reached the front line. Corruption was rife in the rear areas of the White Russian forces. Much of the material supplied by Britain was sold on the black market. While the troops were in rags, fortunes were made in the rear. The equipment for a complete field hospital vanished, including 200 beds. Prostitutes in Novorossisk were wearing British Army nurses' uniforms, while the troops in the front line died for lack of medical attention.

NOTES

[1] National Archives, Mercer, Lieutenant A., log-book
[2] Wrangel, P., *The Memoirs of General Wrangel*, Williams and Norgate, London, 1929, pages 95-96
[3] Quoted in Wrangel, Alexis, *General Wrangel 1878-1929*, Leo Cooper, London, 1987, page 125
[4] National Archives, Cronin, combat report
[5] National Archives, Maund, A. C., report
[6] National Archives, War Office telegrams
[7] National Archives, 47 Squadron diary
[8] National Archives, Mercer, Lieutenant A., log-book
[9] Collishaw, R., 'Memoirs of a Canadian Airman', Roundel, July–Aug, 1964, page 21
[10] Jones, Ira, *An Air Fighter's Scrapbook*, Vintage Aviation Library, London, 1990
[11] National Archives, Training Mission report
[12] National Archives, Grigson. J. W. B., War Experiences
[13] Ibid.

Detail of picture on p. 85.

CHAPTER FOURTEEN

OCTOBER 1919

At the start of the month, the Armed Forces of South Russia continued their advance towards Moscow. The left wing captured the town of Orel on 15 October. They did not know it at the time but this was the high point of the attack. Orel was only 240 miles from Moscow and only 120 miles from Tula, the most important armaments manufacturing centre in Russia. Denikin's advanced patrols came within 160 miles of Moscow. By late in the month, the Red Army leadership had decided to change the main thrust of their counter-attack from the eastern front, where they had been opposed and beaten by General Wrangel, to the western front to protect Moscow.

The Don Cossack Army under General Sidorin also continued to advance, until 24 October, when the Red Army General Budenny with his cavalry corps captured the town of Voronezh, which was on the point of junction between the Volunteer Army and the Don Cossack Army. Forces moved from other fronts had been used to strengthen Budenny, the great Red Army cavalry leader. Although born in the Don Cossack region, Semen Bedenny was never considered a Cossack. He had served in the Tsar's Army for fifteen years and had risen to the rank of sergeant major. Rising through the ranks of the Red Army, by mid-November 1919 he commanded the First Cavalry Army.

The advance of Denikin's forces during the summer and autumn of 1919 had captured vast amounts of territory, but Denikin never had the numbers to control the land he had captured. Once the momentum had gone out of the advance, the White forces were seen to be in a very exposed position. The differences between the various sections of Denikin's forces had remained below the surface while they were winning, but with defeat they came to the surface, causing splits in the White leadership. The social structure of the countryside controlled by the Whites began to collapse as the retreat started.

On the eastern end of the front, General Wrangel continued to fight a series of defensive battles to save Tsaritsin from capture. Throughout the autumn, he had fought against the major Red Army attack on Denikin's Army. Although he was always outnumbered, Wrangel had managed to hang onto Tsaritsin in the face of four major assaults.

With both C and B Flights at the front, the attacks on the Red Army were stepped up. Tsaritsin was still under attack from both the north and south. Red troops, supported by armed trains and gunboats on the river, mounted heavy attacks from the north. On 1 October, two bombing sorties by C Flight were flown against river transport, as well as two sorties by the Camels of B Flight. Early in the month, A Flight's train left Ekaterinodar for Beketovka. It was intended that A Flight would use the DH9As and be under the command of Captain Leonard Horatio Slatter. During the First World War, Slatter had shot down seven German aircraft while flying Sopwith Pups and Camels. He went on to be a squadron leader, and during the Second World War he became the leader of Coastal Command and finally retired as an air marshal.

The White Army planned a major attack on Tcherni-Yar for 3 September. To support this attack, C Flight moved on the night before to the forward base at Viasovka, fifty miles east of their airfield at Beketovka. During the attack, Major Collishaw dropped bombs on a steamboat alongside the wharf at Tcherni-Yar. Later in the day, he hit a gunboat on the river; the vessel was described as lying helpless in the water after the attack. He also hit an ammunition barge, which exploded, damaging a steam tug lying alongside. Captain Kinkead flew three sorties, involving over five hours' flying, and dropped twelve 20 lb bombs on shipping. A DH9A bombed gun emplacements at Tcherni-Yar. During the day, Captain Anderson and his observer Lieutenant Mitchell flew for 9 hours 20 minutes and dropped twelve 122 lb bombs, together with forty-eight 20 lb bombs. A gunboat, a steamboat, and a barge were disabled, and gun emplacements were bombed. But the ground attack on Tcherni-Yar was a failure, as recorded by Anderson:

> The morale of the Russian Army after over five years of war was appallingly bad. I am convinced that attacks were successful when the defenders decided it was best to retreat. In this case retreat was impossible as the town was surrounded and the attack was a miserable failure. No sign of life could be seen in or around the town and I am convinced that anything like a determined attack would have been successful.[1]

RAF personnel, photographed at Ekaterinodar. Front row: Doc Murphy, 'Seedy' Brougal, Sam Kinkead, unknown Russian, Walter Anderson, Doc Flood. Back row: Captain Smith, Jock Mitchell, Tommy Thompson, 'Gus' Edwards, 'Sporty' Murton, unknown Russian interpreter.

After the failure to take Tcherni-Yar, the White Army retreated to within thirty miles of Tsaritsin. During the day, 47 Squadron flew 33 hours and 50 minutes on operations.

Captain Kinkead and Captain Burns-Thomson carried out further raids on the river traffic the next day, and on 5 October bombed artillery that was shelling the White forces. Captain Anderson and Lieutenant Cronin, flying two DH9s, also bombed an artillery battery and obtained a direct hit with a 112 lb bomb. On 6 October, Captains Grigson and Keymer, with observers Lieutenants Thompson and Aten (Aten was officially a pilot), attacked an armoured train. At low level, the train was hit by 112 lb and 20 lb bombs. High casualties were reported. Other sorties against the river traffic were mounted in the afternoon. A night raid on the gunboats at Dubovka was carried out by Captain Anderson, flying a DH9 escorted by Captains Kinkead and Burns-Thomson, and several were hit.

On 7 October, Captain Burns-Thomson and Captain Kinkead were credited with shooting down two Red air force aircraft, as detailed in the combat report:

> While escorting DH9s on a raid on Dubovka Capt. Kinkead and myself engaged two Nieuports. Capt Kinkead attacked one. I attacked the other

one driving both machines on to the ground. Neither of the machines put up a fight at all.[2]

Also on 7 October, A Flight's train finally left Ekaterinodar for the front.

More bombing raids were carried out on 8 and 9 October by DH9s and DH9As, but there only seem to have been two Camels in flying condition on any one day. Major Collishaw claimed to have shot down a Red air force Albatross D-V while flying one of B Flight Camels:

> Flying Camel 6396, I had several encounters with enemy pilots and on October 9 I sent an Albatross D-V bearing Red markings down out of control about 20 miles North of Tsaritsin, being able to follow it down and see it crash on one of the banks of the Volga.[3]

No record can be found in the squadron diaries for this enemy aircraft destroyed, but a record in the Canadian Air Warfare Historical Section gives 8 October for this shoot-down.

On 10 October, Captain Keymer, escorted by Captains Kinkead and Burns-Thomson, flying Camels, bombed an armoured train. The train was seen to retire. Besides escorting the bombing aircraft, the Camels each carried four 20 lb bombs. On 10 October, Anderson and Mitchell attacked a Red Army train, causing heavy damage. They went on to attack an enemy artillery battery and, in his usual way, Anderson swooped low over the guns to give a good field of fire to Mitchell. The DH9 was hit by machine-gun fire, wounding Anderson in the arm. After he had managed to land back at Beketovka, Anderson was sent back to hospital for the rest of the month. Captain Anderson, along with his observer Mitchell, seems to have carried out more operations than any other member of 47 Squadron. Also on 10 October, Lieutenants A. H. Day and R. Addison were awarded the DFC for attacks on riverboats. The DH9As were able to carry 230 lb bombs, and these were used on shipping raids to good effect.

During the second week in October, Major Collishaw was diagnosed as having typhoid and was sent back by train to hospital in Ekaterinodar, accompanied by two of the squadron ground crew who were also sick. During the train trip, the two ground crew became so ill with dysentery they were unable to stand. Collishaw also became so sick he was taken off the train by the Russian rail authorities and left in the care of an elderly Russian woman, who looked after him in her own house. For several weeks, the RAF authorities completely lost track of Collishaw during the confusion that was building up across the Russian countryside. When he was finally tracked down, and well enough to be moved, he was transferred to a Russian hospital.

On 11 October, A and C Flights carried out more raids on the Volga gunboat fleet and troop concentrations. Captain Keymer and Lieutenant Thompson bombed a gun battery, causing heavy damage, and during the same flight attacked 1,000 cavalry with bombs and then descended to low level and fired 500 rounds of small arms ammunition. In the course of the day, Captain Kinkead and Burns-Thomson each carried out six sorties against enemy troops, dropping forty-eight 20 lb bombs and notching up a total of 5 hours and 40 minutes flying time each.

The Red Army had stepped up its attacks on the Tsaritsin front, and on 12 October a large force of Red cavalry allegedly under the command of General Dumenko broke through at the junction between Wrangel's Caucasian Army and the Don Cossack Army. This force then swept round and advanced on Tsaritsin from the west. If this force had achieved its objective, then 47 Squadron at Beketovka would have been cut off, along with the rest of the Caucasian Army. But B Flight carried out a series of attacks in conjunction with the Caucasian Army cavalry under General Ulagai, forcing the Red cavalry to retreat. The Squadron diary for 12 October reads:

Capts. Kinkead and Burns Thompson raided troops in the Kotluban region and after disposing of eight 20Lb. Bombs they dived to within 10 feet of the ground and machine gunned a large force of enemy cavalry about to attack. The whole force rapidly retreated with many casualties, and great panic. Capt. Kinkead's machine and engine were hit with rifle fire. 1400 rounds of S.A.A. fired.[4]

Only two Camels flew on 12 October (it is not recorded, but the other Camels must be presumed to have been unserviceable). An RAF report sent by Colonel Maund described their exploits:

Crack Bolshevik cavalry division broke through Don troops and turned left flank Volunteer Army. British pilots on Camels led by Capt. Kinkead attacked same and dispersed them in panic saving critical situation. Bolshevik cavalry Division since withdrawn from Caucasian Don front. Russians Delighted with work.[5]

Captain Kinkead was awarded a DFC for his work on 12 October. Much has been written about this incident. Lieutenant Aten claimed to have taken part in the attack and that four Camels were involved. He also claimed that 1,600 casualties were inflicted on the Red Cavalry. This is just not credible. In reality, only two aircraft were involved and only 1,400 rounds fired in total. The claim that the Red cavalry attack by General

Dumenko and 4,000 troops were turned back by two aircraft is the stuff of legend. Kinkead undoubtedly led an effective attack carried out at low level and disrupted the cavalry advance, but it was General Ulagai and the Kuban Cossack Cavalry that routed General Dumenko and drove back his forces.

The White troops on the Tsaritsin front continued to be under heavy attack. During the rest of the month, the attacks by 47 Squadron on the Red Army and the shipping on the Volga continued. Lieutenants Cronin and Hatchett attacked an armoured train on 13 October. Captain Daley obtained a hit on a barge on 14 October. Captain Frogley was awarded the Distinguished Service Order for work he carried out on 15 October, as described in the citation:

> A fleet of about forty Bolshevik vessels armed with all description of guns, having broken through the defences of the Volunteer Army commenced a bombardment of Tsaritsin. Captain Frogley led a formation of machines on 15th October 1919 and at a height of 1,000 feet dropped his bombs with such effect that the fleet was dispersed – several vessels having been destroyed.[6]

The B Flight Camels were not always successful. On 16 October, Captains Kinkead and Daley, with Lieutenant Aten, bombed cavalry with no observed results.

A forward airfield at Kotluban was created for B Flight to give them the range to operate further behind enemy lines, the Camels not having the range of the DH9s. Kotluban was on the rail line thirty miles north-west of Tsaritsin. Flying from Kotluban on 17 October, Captains Kinkead, Burns-Thomson, and Daley bombed an artillery battery, putting it out of action. In the later part of the month, an average of three Camels a day were serviceable and they seem to have specialised in attacking Army targets, while A and C Flights attacked Volga shipping. Captains Kinkead, Burns-Thomson, and Daley carried out sorties on each day until 24 October, attacking artillery, bridges, and road transport. Captain Grigson and his observer, Lieutenant E. G. T. Chubb, were awarded the DFC for work they carried out between 20 and 23 October. The citation for Grigson reads:

> For conspicuous gallantry and devotion to duty at Tsaritsin, October 20th to 23rd, Captain Grigson carried out 20 bomb raids against the enemy fleet of 40 vessels on the Volga River bombarding Tsaritsin. He destroyed four gunboats and his splendid work led to the repulse of the fleet.[7]

Captain Keymer and his observer, Lieutenant Thompson, both died on 24 October when their bombs exploded as they were taking off, completely wrecking the aircraft and killing the two officers. General Holman and Colonel Maund visited the squadron on 22 October and stayed until the end of the month. On 26 October, both of these visitors took part in operations, flying as observers during attacks on the river barges at Dubovka.

B Flight's train moved to the advanced airfield at Kotluban on 31 October. During the visit by General Holman, seven of the aircrew were awarded DFCs, while Captains Kinkead and Frogley were given the DSO. The pilots and observers of C Flight had been in combat for five months and it was decided to disband the flight, with some of its members leaving for good and some going on leave. Some did volunteer to stay in Russia. Its DH9s were handed over to the Russian squadron operating at Beketovka. During the month, it was claimed that fifteen river steamers had been sunk, forcing the remainder to pull back north out of range of the squadron. Soviet records dispute the number of boats actually sunk, but admit that a large number were damaged or sunk. The Soviet view was that in late October early freezing forced the gunboat fleet to pull back north to their winter quarters at Lower Novgorod. If the boats had been trapped in a frozen River Volga close to Tsaritsin, Wrangel's cavalry would have soon crossed the ice and eliminated them.

In terms of the weight of bombs dropped, October had been the busiest month for the squadron during the time it operated in Russia. During the month, 37,206 lbs of bombs were dropped, including eleven 230 lb bombs. In addition, 14,000 rounds of ammunition were fired during the course of 228 hours and 50 minutes of operational flying. A further 36 hours and 35 minutes were taken up with test flying.

Back home in Britain, there had been growing opposition to the Allied intervention in the Russian Civil War. To placate this movement, it was proposed to make 47 Squadron part of the Training Mission. But Maund, who had been recently promoted to Acting Brigadier General, protested and stated that they had 'gone to Russia to fight' (although he himself only appears to have taken part in one operation). To hide the real nature of 47 Squadron's work, it was renamed a 'detachment' and was shown on paper as part of the Training Mission. All the squadron members were required to sign a declaration that they were volunteers.

J. E. Hodgson, a journalist, interviewed General Wrangel in Tsaritsin. In a book he wrote later, he stated:

Wrangel told me that time after time they (47 Squadron) had saved his Army. Our men once located a battery of twenty three limbers and, flying very low, in a very few minutes wiped out all the gun crews, and every horse but one, within full view of the White Army.[8]

It may be true that Wrangel said this to Hodgson, but Wrangel made no mention of the RAF in his memoirs published in 1929. Hodgson later also wrote:

> I saw one communist soldier, wearing a red shirt which made him an easy mark, run behind a tree in the hope of escaping a pursuing plane. The machine sailed three times round the tree before it found itself able to shoot with effect.[9]

This has the ring of an apocryphal story, Hodgson may have listened to one too many pilots' tales.

The Training Mission during October had expanded until it included ten instructors. Thirty-three RE8s had been drawn from the stores at Novorossisk and twenty-six of these had been erected. The aircraft had been delivered in crates. Of these, twenty-two were serviceable. During the month, only two pilots had been sent solo; of these, one had crashed on his second solo after going into a flat spin, and the second had stated that he did not feel comfortable in these machines and did not wish to fly again. Major Archer summarised progress in his report for October:

> The work of equipping and building machines has been fairly rapid and on the whole satisfactory. On the other hand the dual instruction has been most disappointing in its results. The pilots are supposedly skilled pilots, but they are evidently very badly out of practice, and require 5 or 6 hours dual and are then still uncertain. This is beyond the powers and functions of the limited personnel and equipment of this mission, and in consequence the work in this respect has proceeded very slowly. There is also a very marked antipathy to the RE8 which greatly impedes progress.[10]

A number of White air force units were equipped with the RE8, but very little was achieved with the aircraft and a number of crashes occurred.

During October, a young Red Army cavalry sergeant was fighting in the Tsaritsin area. He later wrote:

> Here at Tsaritsin, at Bakhtiyarovka and Zaplavnoye, our 14th Cavalry Regiment also squared off against the enemy's Caucasian Army. We could distinctly hear the endless shelling in the Tsaritsin area and at the approaches to the city from Kamyshin. Heavy losses were being inflicted

on the enemy, but our troops too, were being badly bled. In hand to hand fighting with White Kalmyk troops between Zaplavnoye and Achtuba [both on the east bank of the Volga just south of Tsaritsin] I was wounded when a hand grenade exploded. The splinters went deep into my left side and thigh, and I was sent to the hospital, where I again succumbed to a bout of typhus.[11]

The young Red soldier recovered and went on to become the greatest military leader of the twentieth century, Marshal Zhukov.

NOTES

[1] National Archives, Anderson, W. F., War Experiences
[2] National Archives, Burns-Thomson, W., combat report
[3] Collishaw, Raymond, *Air Command*, William Kimber, London, 1972, page 201
[4] National Archives, 47 Squadron diary
[5] National Archives, Maund, A. C., report
[6] National Archives, Frogley, S. G., medal citation
[7] National Archives, Grigson, J. W. B., medal citation
[8] Hodgson, J. E., *With Denikin's Armies*, London, 1923
[9] Ibid.
[10] National Archives, Archer, J. O., report
[11] Zhukov, Marshal G. K., memoirs

Detail of picture on p. 96.

CHAPTER FIFTEEN

NOVEMBER 1919

Although Denikin had been forced to retreat from Orel by the start of November, the position on the western and central part of the front did not appear to be beyond recovery for the Armed Forces of South Russia. Denikin still hoped that he would be able to recover the situation and continue the advance on Moscow. In reality, there was little chance of this happening. By late autumn, the Red Army had nearly doubled the number of troops they had facing the southern front.

The advance during the summer and early autumn by General Denikin's Army had captured an enormous amount of territory but there were simply not enough troops available to police this area. Behind the front line there were bands of deserters, from both sides, who took control of towns or even complete areas of the countryside. The Ukrainian nationalist Petlyura carried out attacks on the White forces. Makhno, who changed sides a number of times, was organising a guerrilla force behind the White lines and at one moment threatened to capture Taganrog. All these different groups, plus Red government supporters, turned the White Armies' rear area into an uncontrollable combat zone. The whole area was degenerating into anarchy. Denikin was forced to pull troops he could ill-afford to lose out of the front line in an attempt to control the rear areas.

General Wrangel continued to hold onto Tsaritsin, and during the month managed to advance a short distance and capture Dubovka. But, on 28 November, General Budenny and the Red Cavalry Army started an attack on the northern front that led to a forty-day Soviet advance.

The weather in November closed in and did not allow much flying during the month. In addition, there were now only A and B Flights at the front. On 2 November, three of B Flight's Camels flew up to join their train at Kotluban. They were followed on 3 November by Lieutenant Aten, flying the fourth Camel. The next day, the Camels flew three sorties in the morning and two in the afternoon, attacking Red Army targets. No flying was possible on 5 and 6 November because of bad weather. On 7 November, two new DH9As were flown up to Beketovka. On 10 November, Captains Kinkead and Daley, with Lieutenant Aten, carried out an attack on enemy road transport. The condition of the four Camels continued to decline and it was an effort to keep them flying. During the attack on 10 November, Captain Kinkead's controls jammed and turned the Camel on its back. He only recovered control at 200 ft from the ground.

The DH9s used by C Flight were given to a White Russian squadron operating at the front. The train used by C Flight was driven back to Ekaterinodar. The squadron diary for 10 November reads:

> C Flight Officers and Other Ranks proceeded to Novorossisk to await embarkation on leave.[1]

Anderson returned to service on 10 November and was given command of a 'new' C Flight that was being formed, using RE8 aircraft. The DH9s used a water-cooled engine and were nearly impossible to keep running in the frozen Russian winter conditions; RE8s were equipped with an air-cooled engine, more suited to the prevailing weather. Eight brand-new RE8s in crates were issued to Captain Anderson, to be used by the reconstituted C Flight. Anderson took command of the train used by the 'old' C Flight and began to gather together the necessary men and materials.

Bad weather again prevented flying until 12 November, when Captain Langley, flying a DH9A from Beketovka, bombed three columns of infantry near the village of Prishibo, scattering the troops. Three of B Flight's Camels set off to bomb enemy cavalry close to the Don River, but Captain Burns-Thomson was forced to turn back with engine trouble. No flying was possible on 13 November, and the following day Captain Kinkead and Lieutenant Aten were forced to turn back because of bad weather. Weather conditions again stopped flying on 15 November, but Captain Grigson flew one sortie with a DH9A on 16 November. Road transport was bombed and several barges being unloaded on the Volga were machine-gunned. Captains Kinkead and Burns-Thomson set out to bomb enemy cavalry, but Burns-Thomson was again forced to turn back to Kotluban because of engine trouble. On 17 November, Kinkead and Burns-Thomson bombed troops and road transport.

On 18 November, two DH9As, flown by Captains Grigson and Langley, bombed the village of Rahinka and claimed to have demolished many houses. Captains Kinkead and Daley bombed and machine-gunned troops near the village of Loznoe. When they returned, they reported that the enemy was advancing all along the front. No flying was possible on 19 and 20 November because of bad weather. On 21 November, Captain Grigson and his observer, Lieutenant Chubb, bombed enemy troops and attacked an enemy aircraft seen on the ground at Kolobobka. The DH9A was hit by ground fire and the main fuel tank started to leak, forcing them to return. They reported that the White Army was seen to be in full retreat. Captains Kinkead and Daley, with the Russian pilot Lieutenant Grigorieff, attacked an armoured train with 20 lb bombs. Captain Kinkead claimed a direct hit. Later in the day, Kinkead and Daley bombed enemy troops and transport. The Russian pilot Grigorieff had been in nominal command of the B Flight train since it was formed. Lieutenant Aten later stated that Grigorieff developed typhus and was killed when the hospital in Rostov he was recovering in was captured by Red forces and burned to the ground.

No flying was possible after 21 November. It had been decided to move A and B Flights to the Kharkov front. This plan was put into operation at the moment the White forces were starting to collapse all along the front. The headquarters train arrived at Beketovka on 21 November to help with the move by the two flights. This train was made up of two dozen coaches and contained the administrative staff for the squadron, plus a small amount of spares and equipment. On 24 November, the redoubtable Captain Anderson arrived back at Beketovka with the C Flight train. The brand-new RE8s in crates, the ones the Russians had finally refused to use, were carried by the train up to Beketovka to be assembled.

B Flight's train and aircraft returned to Beketovka from Kotluban on 26 November and left for the Kharkov front on 27 November. Major Collishaw left hospital and returned to Beketovka that same day and resumed command of the squadron. During the rest of the month, A Flight aircraft were dismantled and loaded onto the flat-bed trucks that were part of their train. The squadron (now 'A Detachment') had dropped 4,508 lbs of bombs and fired 3,400 rounds of machine-gun ammunition during 62 hours and 55 minutes of flying time during November.

General Maund produced a report in November stating the hardships that the RAF men were working under:

> The strain on Personnel is very great. Always bad at heavy manual labour, the trained mechanic is spending most of his time loading and unloading trains. Great hardships prevail. Active service life on the Western Front [Maund served on the Western Front in the same squadron as Albert Ball in 1916] is like living in the lap of luxury when compared with campaigning in winter time in Russia. Quarters are crowded and uncomfortable, being in railway rolling stock. Food is monotonous – there is a constant fight against cold. Mail is at most irregular and unsatisfactory.[2]

Things were going to get even worse for the RAF as the Volunteer Army began to collapse.

The RAF Training Mission in Taganrog continued to try and teach the Russians to fly the RE8s during November. News began to reach the mission that the units which had been equipped with the RE8 were not using the aircraft at the front. It was decided that all the DH9s used by 47 Squadron, plus the ones in storage, would be handed over to the Russians, as they seemed to have no problems with that type of aircraft. The British pilots would use the remaining RE8s. It was also thought that during the winter the air-cooled engines of the RE8s would operate better than the water-cooled DH9s. Makhno, who was usually described as a bandit, captured an area close to Taganrog, threatening General Denikin's HQ, and was bombed by instructors from the Training Mission flying RE8s.

During the last week of November, General Maund authorised the creation of another flight of British aircraft to work at the front. This was to be known as Z Flight, and was formed from the instructors at the Training Mission. A lot has been written about Z Flight. It has been called secret, clandestine, or undercover. But, in reality, the Training Mission had nothing to do now that they had finally abandoned the attempt to teach the Russians to fly the RE8, and a number of these aircraft were available. Also, the Armed Forces of South Russia were under severe pressure on the Kharkov front. It made sense to send another flight of aircraft to the front using available pilots and aircraft. Z Flight was to be commanded by Major Archer, an experienced pilot, and senior to Collishaw.

In his orders setting up the flight, Maund stated that the Russians would provide the necessary rolling stock to create the train the flight would need. The train would carry the fuel, oil, spares, munitions, and food for one month. Personnel included six pilots, six observers, and seven other officers. Also on the strength of the flight were twenty-six other ranks and fourteen Russians. The train provided by the Russians arrived at the Baltic Works in Taganrog on 30 November and the loading of stores started.

NOTES

[1] National Archives, 47 Squadron diary
[2] National Archives, Maund, A. C., report

CHAPTER SIXTEEN

DECEMBER 1919

The general Red Army advance continued at the start of December. General Budenny was advancing into the junction between the Don Army and the Volunteer Army. Wrangel was forced to fall back to the outskirts of Tsaritsin and to evacuate the east bank of the Volga. General Denikin, in his headquarters at Tagenrog, still thought that he could save the situation. Most of the available tanks, around forty, and most of the available aircraft were to be concentrated north-east of Kharkov at Valuiki. He also tried to place five cavalry divisions at Valuiki to mount a counter-attack. These included a cavalry corps that he withdrew from General Wrangel's Caucasian Army, a cavalry division from the Don Army, and a Terek cavalry division that had been fighting against Makhno. But Denikin did not act fast enough, and the Red Army advance had captured this area before he could concentrate his forces.

In the middle of the month, Denikin sacked General Mai-Maevsky, who seemed to have lost his grip on the situation. Wrangel was appointed to command the entire front on 8 December, but it was now too late for any one person to save the day. Wrangel accused both General Mamontov and Shkuro of disobeying orders, removed them from command, and replaced them with General Ulagai. On 11 December, Kharkov fell to the Red Army and the retreat continued. By the end of the month, the Armed Forces of South Russia were only just holding onto Tagenrog, Rostov, and Novocherkassk, the Don Cossack capital. The front had collapsed into compete chaos as thousands fled. In one month, the Army had lost the ground it had captured in the last eight months. At the end of the month, Denikin sacked Wrangel, just over two weeks after appointing him.

After leaving Beketovka, B Flight's train arrived at Valuiki, on the Kharkov front, on 1 December, but they were forced to retreat immediately because of the Red Army advance. B Flight moved back to Kupyansk, which is south-east of Kharkov. Also on 1 December, the headquarters train and the A Flight train left Beketovka. On 4 December, B Flight moved back to Peschanoe, where they were joined by the headquarters and the A Flight train on 7 December. Two of the Camels had been reassembled by 8 December, and Captains Kinkead and Daley attacked enemy troop concentrations in the Urasov area and scattered them in disorder. The report reads:

> At Valuiki town deserted, except for hostile cavalry patrol – 500 enemy infantry with machine guns and considerable transport entered Valuiki ... East of Kozynka 500 enemy cavalry moving south east with considerable transport. Both pilots attacked two columns with machine gun fire from a very low altitude, completely dispersing them in panic in all directions and destroying a great many. An AA gun was encountered with this column ... All movements towards the South. No Volunteer forces observed within area of Bolshevik cavalry.[1]

In reality, the two flights had arrived at the moment the White Volunteer Army was facing complete collapse. On 9 December, the two flights moved back to Savatovo but were again forced to retire the following day. An airfield was established south of Kremennaya, at Rubejnaia, on 11 December. The Camels used by B Flight were now judged to be completely unserviceable and the flight was told to retire to Tagenrog to refit. The airfield at Tagenrog had been stocked with equipment to support the expected advances on the Kharkov front.

Z Flight's train had finished loading supplies on 1 December and had left Taganrog in the company of the British Military Mission headquarters train. By 3 December, Z Flight had reached Kupyansk and spent the day on the same airfield as B Flight. But when B Flight moved to Peschanoe, Z Flight moved south to Kislovka. The White Russian No. 6 Squadron, flying Camels, was also based at Kislovka. It proved difficult to find suitable landing grounds next to railway sidings. The weather during this period was hard frost with snow and low cloud and mist – very poor flying weather.

Z Flight erected their wireless station on 7 December and contacted Taganrog to send the aircraft up to the train. There was a break in the weather on 9 December, which was described as fine and bright, and seven RE8s left Taganrog for the Z Flight train. One of them was flown by Captain Smith, who had General Holman as his observer. One RE8 carried out a forced landing and did not arrive until the following day. After he had delivered his passenger, Captain Smith flew back to Taganrog, leaving six RE8s to be used by Z Flight, including the one that had made a forced landing. Also on 9 December, a Sopwith Camel of the No. 6 Russian Squadron crashed and the pilot was killed.

One of the pilots in Z Flight, Lieutenant Vic Clow, later claimed that Z Flight had planned to bomb Moscow with two aircraft. Kislovka is around 380 miles from Moscow, so this may have been a little optimistic for the RE8s. The plan was to establish a base well behind Red Army lines on the largely empty steppes and fly in a supply of fuel to allow the two attacking aircraft to refuel on the way to Moscow and on the way back. But permission was never granted. The Military Mission had been specifically banned from attacking Moscow in September. Christopher Dobson and John Miller, in their book *The Day We Almost Bombed Moscow*, describe how the men of Z Flight would sit round a campfire in the evenings at Valuiki listening to a wind-up gramophone. This is complete fantasy. Z Flight never reached Valuiki and the idea of anyone sitting round a campfire in the frozen depths of a Russian winter is a little hard to accept. They also describe how the RAF men had fishing rods with them to add to their rations. Any water on the steppes was frozen solid.

The weather on 10, 11, and 12 December was again impossible for flying, with fog and mist. The Squadron diary for Z Flight on 10 December states:

> Considerable uneasiness on the part of the Russians as an enemy cavalry group is reported on the right flank. Flight urged to leave, by Railway Authorities, but in view of the fact that the weather is impossible for aeroplanes, it was decided to stay in hope of weather becoming fit for flying ... General Holman remained on Z Flight train.[2]

On 11 December, Major Archer decided he could wait no longer and the six RE8s were dismantled and placed on the rail flatcars. The train left in the afternoon. An airfield at Kubane was found to be unsuitable and the train retired again to Rubejnaia, arriving on 13 December. The weather was described as intense cold. A temporary hangar was erected and two machines unloaded.

General Maund rebuked Major Collishaw for sending B Flight back to Taganrog, sending him the following message:

> On whose authority was 'B' Flight ordered to return from the front to Taganrog. You are authorised to move your flights where necessary for carrying on campaign but you may not remove them from the front without orders from here.[3]

As B Flight's train and aircraft had already left, there was not much that could be done about it. General Holman had travelled with the Z Flight train as they moved back again to the same field at Rubyansk as A Flight. On 14 December, after the DH9As of A Flight had been re-erected, Major Collishaw, with General Holman as observer, bombed an armoured train near Urasov. General Holman signed the combat report, which stated:

> Soviet Cavalry and transport to strength of 1 regt. were entering Urasov at 1430 hours. Urasov and neighbouring villages appear to be occupied by a large number of Soviet troops. Unfavourable weather conditions this morning prevented a more complete reconnaissance.[4]

Z Flight's diary for 14 December reads:

> "A" Flight has got one aeroplane (a DH9A) serviceable, and General Holman went off as an observer on a reconnaissance, doing some bombing, which was afterwards found to be on friendly troops. Fortunately, no casualties. The mixed up state of enemy and friendly troops makes it quite impossible to say who they may be, and, in consequence, bombing, during the movement, becomes very hazardous. Orders issued not to bomb for the present unless the situation is such that there is no possibility of mistake.[5]

Neither Collishaw nor General Holman mentions the bombing of friendly troops.

The mechanics of Z Flight managed to get one aircraft ready on 15 December, but when a reconnaissance was attempted the engine refused to start because of the intense cold. On 16 December, another RE8 was erected. One successful reconnaissance was carried out, but the first RE8 was still having engine trouble and only managed one circuit of the airfield before landing. On 17 December, one aircraft tried to carry out a reconnaissance on three occasions but was forced back by bad weather each time. General Holman was again in the air as an observer on 18 December, with Lieutenant Bains as pilot. The RE8 carried out a reconnaissance of the Starobyelsk area, but no enemy were seen. In the afternoon of 18 December, another flight was attempted but the RE8 crashed and was destroyed, though the pilot and observer survived.

With A Flight on 16 December, Lieutenant Villa returned from a reconnaissance with the news that the Volunteer Army was in full retreat. Captains Grigson and Breakey, flying two DH9As, with Captain Gordon and Lieutenant Spalton as observers, bombed Soviet forces on 17 December, as recorded in combat report:

2.30 pm Tarasovka, Continuous stream of transport (horse) along road with intervals between groups which were 50–100 strong. Bombs dropped. Direct hit on wagon. AA Battery firing from this vicinity. Troops shot at and bombed ... Preebrajennoe, About 500 cavalry. Machine gunned by our machines. About 2,000 cavalry and infantry moving South along both sides of railway.[6]

The local Russian commanding officer was General Ulagai, and Major Collishaw provided him with information after a reconnaissance on 18 December. As the Red Army advanced closer, A Flight and the headquarters train were forced to retreat to Popasnaya on 19 December. Three machines took off from Rubejnaia, carried out an operation, one of them carrying General Holman, and landed at Popasnaya. They reported that the Volunteer Army was still rapidly retreating. The way the squadron retirements were carried out was for an aircraft to find a flat area close to railway sidings in the general area required. The train would pull back to the sidings and the aircraft would fly there, if still serviceable, and land next to the train.

Z Flight also began to fall back on 19 December to the same airfield as A Flight at Popasnaya. Two serviceable RE8s flew off in the morning, and the train left in the afternoon. When Z Flight's train arrived at Popasnaya on 20 December, the aircraft were not there. They arrived later, having been forced by bad weather to spend the night on a stretch of clear ground, the two aircraft having to be tied down because of high winds. During the day, an RE8 flew up from Taganrog, piloted by Captain Smith, to take General Holman back to Taganrog. No flying by Z Flight took place on 21 December. The weather was described as mist and low cloud. Two reconnaissance sorties were attempted on 22 December, but both aircraft soon returned, reporting that they ran into snow ten miles north of the airfield. General Ulagai had ordered another move to the south as the Red Army advanced. Both the serviceable RE8s flew in the afternoon to a landing ground at Krinichnaya. The train also left in the evening, but made very poor progress as rail lines were becoming jammed with retreating troops and refugees. During the night, the train was hit by another train, smashing five of the trucks carrying stores. It was 24 December before the train arrived at Krinichnaya, and it was found that both of the RE8s had been wrecked by high winds the day before. The aircraft had been picketed down, but this had not stopped the damage occurring.

During the last few days of the year, the weather restricted flying. A Flight managed to fly one sortie on 21 December, with Captain Slatter and Lieutenant Spalton, but this was cut short due to bad weather. Two sorties were flown on 22 December. On 23 December, Captain Slatter and

Captain Breakey, flying two DH9As, carried out a reconnaissance flight. Captain Slatter's report read:

> All roads leading to Nesvyetevich from the North Side of river are full of cavalry and transport. The bridge over the Donets river, vicinity of Rubejnaia, intact and in the hands of the enemy. Two armoured trains with cavalry screens are moving south down the railway. Enemy cavalry detachments, carrying Red Flag were in the streets of Lisichansk. In the vicinity of Lisichansk enemy cavalry and infantry approaching from the north towards a foot bridge crossing the river at three points.[7]

The closeness of the enemy forces was reported to the White Russian troops. During the reconnaissance, Captain Breakey and his observer Gordon were hit by ground fire and had to carry out a forced landing close to the Bolshevik forces. They burned their aircraft and returned to A Flight on foot, arriving on 24 December. On Christmas Eve, the headquarters train and A Flight train moved back to Krinichnaya, followed by the remaining two serviceable aircraft after they had carried out another reconnaissance. All three RAF trains at the front were again on the same airfield.

By now, the entire front was in complete collapse. The rail lines were choked solid with dozens of retreating troop trains and trains carrying fleeing civilians. No flying was possible on 25, 26, or 27 December, because of bad weather. Z Flight's diary for Christmas Day reads:

> Strong Wind; cloudy and cold. Christmas dinner for men was a great success, all eating prodigiously waited on by officers, and day passed off well.[8]

On Boxing Day night, the carriage carrying the officers' quarters on the A Flight train caught fire and was burnt out, destroying all their kit. The Z Flight train was next to the burning coach and only just moved in time. Major Collishaw had bought a diamond from a wealthy Russian, who wanted the money to leave the country, and this was lost in the fire. It was now obvious that the squadron would have to retreat into the Caucasus, where they had started from six months earlier, to avoid being cut off. The way into the Caucasus was over the River Don rail bridge at Rostov. B Flight had been at Taganrog, attempting to re-equip with aircraft from the stocks held there. On 28 December, the headquarters train, A Flight train, and Z Flight train were ordered to retreat to Taganrog. The one remaining serviceable RE8 was also flown back to Taganrog. By this stage, there were at least eighty civilian refugees on the Z Flight train.

The headquarters train was joined onto a part of the A Flight train. What was left of A Flight and the enlarged headquarters train separated for the trip. Captain Slatter and his observer Hesketh stayed behind at Popasnaya in order to fly a DH9A to Taganrog, but the aircraft's propeller came to pieces in flight, forcing a landing north of Taganrog, where they finally arrived on 29 December. Major Collishaw was with the enlarged headquarters train, the first of the RAF trains to reach the railway junction at the town of Ilovaiskaia, on 30 December. Here, the train was not allowed entry and forced to turn west away from Taganrog and Rostov towards the Crimea.

The second A Flight train and Z Flight became separated on the trip towards Ilovaiskaia. General Holman had again returned to the front, and his train was travelling with the Z Flight train. Both trains were held up outside Ilovaiskaia, and General Holman and Major Archer walked fourteen miles into the town. The officer in charge of the rail lines, who had already forced Collishaw to turn west for the Crimea, did not want to let the British trains through, but the presence of the corps commander, General Kutypov, and General Holman, forced the issue and the trains were allowed past. The author of a later report on why Collishaw's train was sent to the Crimea stated that:

> From subsequent events I am of the opinion that Railway subordinates acting directly, or indirectly, under anti-British influence, selected a circuitous route, and perhaps with malice of forethought, separated this train from other British units, finally sending it down towards the Crimea.[9]

The Russian in charge of military traffic in Ilovaiskaia was a Colonel Zamarev. He is thought to have been later court-martialled. Z Flight's train arrived in Ilovaiskaia during the morning, but the engine was then stolen for the train carrying the Russian air force's No. 6 Squadron and, despite an argument, they would not return it, even though General Holman tried to intervene. The White Army's discipline was breaking down and the retreat was degenerating into chaotic flight. Another engine was obtained and the train left Ilovaiskaia during the afternoon. As the train left, Red Army shells were falling on the town, and a village five miles away could be seen burning in the distance. The diary entry for the first day of the new year states:

> Considerable looting of trains going on, and a fair amount of shooting. All other ranks turned out as guard of "Z" train. Enemy reported to have cut the line 30 miles to the southward.[10]

Just south of Ilovaiskaia, an abandoned train of ninety coaches blocked the line and orders were given to abandon the RAF train and proceed on foot. Just then, a local divisional commander arrived with enough men to force the abandoned train off the rails, allowing Z Flight's train to continue. The second A Flight train had also passed through Ilovaiskaia, heading towards Taganrog.

During the month of December, A Flight and B Flight had flown 52 hours.

Captain Anderson and C Flight stayed at Beketovka and worked to get the new aircraft into serviceable condition:

> In due course we received eight new RE8s in cases and in ten days we had one in the air. I consider this no small achievement under the circumstances, as it must be remembered that we had no hangar or shelter of any kind, also there was over a foot of snow on the ground and the temperature was never above zero. The day after the first flight we were ordered to prepare for an immediate retreat. As the weather was very uncertain this meant dismantling the machine and putting it on a flat truck. This was very disheartening to the men who had worked so well erecting it.[11]

C Flight spent the rest of the month trying to fall back to Ekaterinodar.

The experience of the British tank school in south Russia during December matched that of the RAF. As the retreat degenerated into a route, the small numbers of tanks available had little effect along a 1,000-mile front line. All the teaching at the tank school was handed over to the Russians, and the British instructors were sent to the front in an attempt to stabilise the situation. But the outnumbered White Army was going into total collapse, as some units fled from the front. General Holman ordered the Army units back to Taganrog.

When the British tank forces reached Taganrog, there seemed to be little chance of stopping the Red advance, so a general withdrawal to Ekaterinodar, in the north Caucasus, was ordered. General Denikin failed to provide adequate rolling stock to evacuate all the British stockpile of equipment at Taganrog and most of it fell into the hands of the Bolsheviks. The war diary for the tank school on 31 December reads:

> No train was provided by the Volunteer Army for the British Tank Corps detachment. Denikin's staff completed their evacuation today, and apparently left the Tank Corps and other British detachments to escape as best they could.[12]

British tank and RAF personnel left Taganrog in early January 1920. Two British-crewed tanks covered the evacuation for as long as possible.

As the position of the Armed Forces of South Russia collapsed, and the British forces struggled to retreat to Taganrog, General Maund sent a letter dated 22 December to Collishaw, criticising him for his record-keeping. This was just before Collishaw was forced to give orders for the dead to be thrown from his train (see next chapter). Maund also demanded an answer to what became known as the 'Ford tender incident':

> I am still waiting for your report on the Ford tenders incident. Please see that it contains answers to the following points:- 1) How they came into the possession of A Detachment last August. 2) On whose authority. 3) Why they were withheld from your return of transport. 4) Who obliterated identification marks and disguised them, and on whose authority. 5) Who was the transport officer at the time. I want a reply to this at once, as it has been left unanswered too long.[13]

Marion Aten, in his book *Last Train Over Rostov Bridge*, referred to the 'Ford tender incident':

> Early in the year, while Colly [Collishaw] was outfitting the Squadron in Ekaterinodar, the boys had filched the van he spoke of from a warehouse siding. They had painted red crosses on its sides and hidden it in a brothel alley. Nobody ever questioned Red Cross markings Kink [Kinkead] had said. He was right. The van had come in very handy … During the eight hours he was with us, General Maund spent five of them riding around in his pilfered van. He made a special point of commending Hoskins [the senior NCO in B Flight] upon the Ford's excellent condition.[14]

In the massive losses that followed, the Ford (or Fords) was forgotten about.

NOTES

[1] National Archives, 47 Squadron diary
[2] National Archives, Z Flight diary
[3] National Archives, Maund, A. C., report
[4] National Archives, Holman, General H. C., combat report
[5] National Archives, Z Flight diary
[6] National Archives, 47 Squadron diary
[7] Ibid.
[8] National Archives, Z Flight diary
[9] National Archives, Bingham, General, report

[10] National Archives, Z Flight diary
[11] National Archives, Anderson, W. F., War Experiences
[12] National Archives, South Russia Tank Corps war diary
[13] National Archives, Maund, A. C., report
[14] Aten, Marion, *Last Train Over Rostov Bridge*, Cassell, London, 1961, page 123-24

Detail of picture on p. 210.

CHAPTER SEVENTEEN

JANUARY 1920

The Red Army advance continued into the beginning of January. Tsaritsin fell on 3 January, as the remnants of the Caucasian Army tried to retreat to Ekaterinodar. General Budenny attempted to cut the Volunteer Army off from Rostov, but this failed. The Don Cossacks and the Volunteer Army managed to retreat across the Don River at Rostov, into the north Caucasus. Taganrog fell on 4 January; Novocherkassk fell on 6 January; and, on 9 January, the Red Army captured Rostov. At this point, the Red Army was exhausted and as over-stretched as General Denikin's Army had been. A major counter-attack at this time would have had a good chance of success, but the Armed Forces of South Russia were a spent force. The Kuban Cossack governing body was at loggerheads with Denikin and not prepared to do any more.

After waiting for supplies to catch up with them, the Red Army tried to cross the River Don at Rostov but was severely defeated. General Budenny's cavalry suffered heavy casualties. Realising the difficulties of crossing the Don at Rostov, Budenny crossed the river with his cavalry corps farther to the east and tried to swing around behind the remnants of General Denikin's Army. But he was stopped by what was left of the Caucasian Army under General Erdel. Large parts of the White Army had retreated into the Crimea and were holding the Red Army at the narrow isthmus of land connecting the Crimea to the mainland. At the end of January, General Denikin had managed to stop the retreat of his Army, but the position they were in was desperate.

The situation in Taganrog on 1 January was that Captain Kinkead, in command of B Flight, was attempting to get an engine to evacuate B Flight's train before the arrival of the Red cavalry. Also in the same situation were the British Military Mission and the personnel from the tank school. On the rail lines passing through Taganrog were the Z Flight and second A

White Russian army troops leaving the Crimea during the evacuation.

Flight trains. General Denikin had already departed from Taganrog and left the British contingent to fend for themselves. In his memoirs, General Wrangel wrote:

> ...on December 19th [new calendar 1 January], late at night, I reached Taganrog. The depots were on fire, the station full of refugees. Headquarters had left in a great haste without waiting for the completion of the evacuation, which had begun too late. The townsfolk, in a panic, were fleeing in carts and on foot. An English officer found me. He told me that Supreme Headquarters had broken their promise and left without taking with them the staff and archives of the English Mission. I suggested taking the Mission in my train, but there was no room for all the archives, and the Mission felt they had no right to abandon them. I promised to send them a train from Rostov and I did so.[1]

Wrangel sent enough engines for the Military Mission and the tank school. Kinkead also managed to obtain an engine and enough coal for B Flight. There were enormous stocks of British equipment at Taganrog, and an attempt was made to destroy as much as possible to stop it falling into the hands of the Red Army. But it was impossible to destroy all the stocks. The officers with Z Flight had left most of their belongings and kit at Taganrog.

Lieutenant Pyper was made responsible for moving this kit, but there was no room on the British Military Mission train, except for eight sick RAF men. Pyper only just obtained room on the B Flight train for himself and two other officers. Z Flight's kit was left on the platform and looted by Russian civilians and Army men.

The Z Flight train and the second A Flight train met up on the afternoon of 1 January. The second A Flight train was involved in a collision with another train, which wrecked three coaches. During the night, the Z Flight train moved ahead and, on 2 January, it met up with the British Military Mission train. Contact was lost with the second A Flight train and with B Flight. General Holman, with another officer, went in search of the other British evacuees and they were found ten miles behind the Mission train. Although Rostov is only forty miles from Taganrog, it took until 5 January before Z Flight arrived with the Mission train.

Major Jenks was on one of the last trains out of Rostov:

> At Rostov bodies were already hanging from lamp-posts before I left and they were the luckier ones. We had to decide which refugees we could take on one of the last trains out and when we left, in spite of all our efforts, every buffer and square inch of roof was occupied by desperate hangers-on. By morning – this was mid winter in Russia – they'd all gone.[2]

The whole fabric of south Russia was descending into chaos.

On the afternoon of 5 January, Z Flight crossed the Rostov bridge and joined General Denikin at Bataisk, on the south side of the River Don. An airfield was selected next to railway sidings. The traffic on the rail lines into Rostov had become so bad that they were choked solid, trapping the tank school, B Flight, and the second A Flight trains north of the river. By 7 January, Z Flight had unloaded an RE8, number E190, from their train and were trying to rig the aircraft for flying. A first flight took place on 8 January. The RE8 flew for thirty minutes around the neighbourhood and reported gunfire. Z Flight was ordered to pull back to Ekaterinodar on 9 January. To speed things up, the RE8 was despatched by air to Ekaterinodar.

The British trains trapped north of the river were finally abandoned on 9 January, the same day that Rostov was captured, as described in the 47 Squadron diary:

> Captain Slatter, Lieutenants Allsebrook and Hesketh rendered unserviceable all machines and transport under continuous heavy shrapnel fire, before evacuating the train.[3]

General Brough was in charge of the evacuation of Rostov, and he was the one who gave the order to abandon the B Flight, A Flight, and tank school trains. General Maund, the RAF commander, wrote a report on the evacuation of Rostov:

> General Brough was unable to save the two RAF trains standing just a mile and a half from safety, and on the morning of the 9th, ordered the RAF to evacuate their trains. As the Russians had abandoned trains of wounded along side of these two trains, it was impossible to burn them, but all material that could be of any use to the enemy was rendered unserviceable beyond repair ... Shells were already falling in the vicinity when our men left ... having to march they could only take with them what they could carry through heavy snow.[4]

The RAF men had been issued with small arms, and some of the Lewis guns off the aircraft were also carried. Under fire from the Red Army, they marched out of the railway sidings, down a small bluff onto the frozen surface of the River Don, and across to the southern side. They were then forced to march through the snow and freezing cold to the British Military Mission train at Bataisk. Most of the men were then transported by train to the port at Novorossisk, where there were still stocks of equipment, as they had only escaped with the clothes on their backs.

On 11 January, Z Flight's train arrived at Tichoretskaia and found that the RE8 that had been sent on ahead had made a forced landing there:

> Found machine E190 had had a forced landing and machine E298 here with a broken rudder. Started to repair E297. Train ordered to proceed to Ekaterinodar. E190 flew with General Holman (Lt. Wallace Pilot) to Ekaterinodar. And crashed. (No casualties) The aircraft crashed in mist 7 versts from aerodrome Ekaterinodar and was stripped by local inhabitants.[5]

It must be every pilot's nightmare to crash with a general in the back seat.

The train arrived at Ekaterinodar on 15 January and ran into the sidings close to the airfield. The rest of the month was spent trying to rig four RE8s into flying condition. The weather was extremely cold and there was snow lying on the airfield. C Flight reached Ekaterinodar on 23 January and managed to get several of the RE8s into flying condition. B Flight was at Novorossisk for the rest of the month, trying to obtain replacement Camels and a new train.

The A Flight train under the command of Major Collishaw had a nightmare journey after being turned away from Taganrog towards the

Crimea. As the train ran towards the Crimea, enemy forces or Bolshevik supporters constantly fired on it. The Russian train crew had deserted, and RAF personnel were driving the train. Fuel for the engine was scarce. When they stopped to get coal for the engine, the train came under sniper fire. The water for the engine had to be created by melting snow. By now, the train was also carrying hundreds of civilian refugees, many of whom were suffering from typhus. Collishaw ordered that the train could not stop for the dead to be buried, as the ground was frozen rock hard, and that bodies should be thrown from the train. In many cases this was disregarded, helping to spread the disease.

Collishaw claimed in his book *Air Command* that the Red Russian cavalry general Budenny sent an armoured train to follow and capture Collishaw's train. On one occasion, this train came into sight but could not get its reputed armament of a nine-inch gun to bear. How is it possible that Collishaw could know what Budenny was doing? At that moment, Budenny was involved in the capture of Taganrog and Rostov. It is unlikely that he would have become personally involved in the escape of one RAF train.

In several places, the tracks had been torn up and the RAF men were forced to lift sections of track from behind the train to replace the damaged sections in front. When the train was forced to stop for fuel, coal was not always available and wooden railway buildings were smashed up to provide fuel. The RAF men also removed rail track from behind the train to stop pursuit. On 1 January, the pursuing Red Army sent an unmanned train careering along the track into the back of Collishaw's train. The last eight coaches were wrecked and, after everything possible had been salvaged, they were abandoned.

A major area of territory north of the Crimea was in the hands of the Red partisan Makhno. The Lewis guns from the squadron's stores were mounted on the train, and this area was successfully crossed on 3 January. Finally, on 4 January, the train pulled into safety in the Crimea. By 6 January, the train had reached Sevastopol, where fuel for the train and rations for the men were obtained from a British warship in the harbour. On 17 January, the train left Sevastopol to move up to the front line, which had stabilised on the neck of land attaching the Crimea to the rest of Russia. The White Russian authorities had promised to provide aircraft for what was left of A Flight. When the train arrived at Djankoi, however, there were no machines available and the train pulled back to an aircraft park at Simpheropol. Here, on 25 January, they were given two DH9s in a very bad state, and the rest of the month was spent in attempting to restore them to flying condition.

Captain Grigson had travelled with the A Flight train into the Crimea:
The retreat became a rout. Our reserve train with machines and MT

took the Rostov line and were captured. The machines we had with us were flown to Taganrog and captured there. We put a strong guard on our coal wagon and locomotive and eventually reached the Crimea. At Sevastopol where we got a few old DH9s, from a Russian Aircraft Repair Depot. These machines had been given to a Russian Squadron by 221 Squadron nearly a year before and were well and thoroughly crashed by the Russians. Some of the machines had actually taken part in the Constantinople bombing during the war. We were not very pleased with them, but they were better than nothing.[6]

Collishaw claimed that he was carrying out combat sorties from 17 January, but the squadron records show that no flying by A Flight took place during January.

47 Squadron (A Detachment) was now split into two distinct parts. General Maund decided that A Flight, with Collishaw in command, was to be known as the Crimea Group. The other three flights, C Flight, B Flight, and Z Flight, were to be known as the Kuban Group, under the command of Captain Slatter. Z Flight was now under the command of Lieutenant Ritchie. Lieutenant Vic Clow from Z Flight contracted malaria during January and was invalided home to Britain.

Rightly or wrongly, it seems that General Maund was blamed for the substantial loss of aircraft, equipment, and stores at Taganrog. In the middle of January, he was asked to resign by General Holman. General Maund stated that the reason he resigned was to highlight the incompetence of the Russian general in charge of the White air force, General Kravtseyvitch. But this may have been an excuse. In any case, General Tkatcheff, who had commanded a large part of the Imperial air force, replaced General Kravtseyvitch. But, for whatever the reason, on 30 January 1920, General Maund left Russia for Constantinople. He was reduced from acting brigadier general to his substantive rank of major and was replaced by Major Archer as RAF commander in south Russia.

The RAF claims to have 'rendered useless' the equipment lost at Taganrog, but the Soviets state that they did use some of the captured equipment. A list of the material lost at Taganrog included eight RE8s, including five still in crates, six SE5As (these had been delivered months before but never used because the correct propellers could not be obtained), and five Camels, plus a large amount of motor transport and spares. B Flight's train had included five Camels and eight Clerget engines, in addition to the motor transport. The second A Flight train had included five DH9As, spares, and motor transport.

As part of the restructuring, the air park at Novorossisk was to be increased in size to get as many aircraft ready as possible. Acting Major

Tanks being evacuated from Novorossisk to the Crimea in early 1920.

Clemson, who had been part of the Training Mission, was placed in command. Captain Head, also from the Training Mission, was in charge of the airfield at Novorossisk. By 23 January, at least one RE8 had been assembled. Also, eight DH9s and six Avro 504s were stored in crates on the docks at Novorossisk. A decision had been taken to send Avro 504 aircraft to help the Russian training organisation. Captain Kinkead and the rest of the B Flight men were in Novorossisk, trying to re-equip and re-establish the flight after losing all their kit on the train at Rostov. On 15 January, Captain Head requested permission to be married, followed by Captain H. S. (Sporty) Murton on 20 January.

It was decided to move the tank school to the Crimea, where it was thought to be possible to hold out against the Bolshevik advances. Most of the tanks were shipped to the Crimea during February, from the port of Novorossisk.

General Holman, in his report on the retreat, expressed admiration for 'the fighting unit of the RAF who have been to the front':

Their behaviour has been admirable in all respects and I put the fact on record with great pleasure and keen appreciation of their good services.[7]

December and January had been a very trying time for the RAF in south Russia.

NOTES

1   Wrangel, General P., *The Memoirs Of General Wrangel*, Williams and Norgate Ltd, London, 1929, page 119
2   Jenks, Major, unpublished memoirs
3   National Archives, 47 Squadron diary
4   National Archives, Maund, A. C., report on the evacuation of Taganrog
5   National Archives, Z Flight diary
6   National Archives, Grigson, J. W. B., War Experiences
7   National Archives, Holman, General H. C., report

CHAPTER EIGHTEEN

FEBRUARY 1920

The Red Army continued to press the remnants of General Denikin's Army back into the Caucasus during February. General Budenny, with the cavalry corps, was moved to attack the White Army on its right flank. But the White troops were not finished yet. During an attempt to cross the Manych River, Budenny's troops were heavily defeated. This was the same River Manych that General Wrangel had crossed in May 1919 to destroy the 10th Red Army. The Kuban Cossack leadership began to have serious disagreements with General Denikin and large numbers of Kuban troops surrendered to the Red forces. The Don Cossacks, on the other hand, remained loyal to Denikin to the end.

In a last throw, what was left of the Volunteer Army and the Don Cossack troops crossed the frozen River Don and recaptured Rostov on 20 February. But the success was shortlived, as Denikin had no reserves to back up the troops in Rostov. The Red Army recaptured the town on 23 February. Late in the month, General Budenny crossed the Manych River and began to advance down the rail line to Ekaterinodar. After disagreements with General Wrangel, General Denikin sacked him on 23 February and he left for the Crimea, where he owned a house. Wrangel, in his memoirs, claimed he resigned.

The White troops who had retreated into the Crimea continued to hold the Red Army at the easily defended Perekop Isthmus. A Flight was still at Simferopol, trying to get the aircraft they had been given by the Russians into airworthy condition. On 1 February, Captain Breakey and Lieutenant Chubb took off in a DH9 on a reconnaissance flight but soon had to return with the 'rudder badly knocked out of place'. On 3 February, Major Archer, who was now in command of the RAF in south Russia, and Captain Slatter flew a DH9A from Ekaterinodar to the Crimea for talks with Collishaw. They returned the same day. Captain Breakey finally

A Sopwith 1½ Strutter with skis.

managed to carry out a successful flight on 4 February, with Lieutenant
Chubb as his observer, attacking troops in the Perekop sector of the front
with machine-guns.

Bad weather on 5 February forced Breakey to call off a reconnaissance
flight and return to base because of fog and low cloud. On the night of 5
February, the RAF contingent received news that a Bolshevik uprising was
about to take place. The RAF men were armed and spent the night patrolling
around their train, but nothing happened. The same thing occurred on the
night of 9 February, but again nothing happened. Bad weather stopped
any more flying until 13 February. The A Flight train moved forward to
the airfield at Djankoi on 12 February; one DH9 was flown to the new
field on 13 February and the other one on 15 February. The Russians had
provided another DH9, and Lieutenant Langley proceeded to the aircraft
park at Simferopol to fly it back to Djankoi. Captains Grigson and Gordon
carried out a successful flight on 16 February; although the cloud base was
only 300 feet, two 65 lb bombs were dropped on rolling stock to good
effect and horse transport on a road was fired on, causing panic.

The Red air force mounted two bombing raids on Djankoi on 17
February. Only four small bombs were dropped: two failed to explode and
two missed the intended targets. A Flight sustained no damage. Captains
Grigson and Gordon were in the air again on 18 February. The railway
station at Novo-Aleksyeevka was bombed with sixteen 20 lb bombs. The
station was full of rolling stock; direct hits were obtained and several

buildings were set on fire. Inaccurate AA fire was seen from an armoured train in the station. Grigson's combat report reads:

> Combats in the Air. A Flight, 18/2/20, 1520hrs. DH9 2874. Novo-Aleksyeevka, Armament 1 Vickers and 1 Lewis, Height 2,000-3,000ft. Pilot Capt J. W. B. Grigson, Observer Captain C. F. Gordon, Result – Driven down 2 miles S. W. of Novo-Aleksyeevka. Type 1 and a 1/2 Sopwith Strutter fitted with skis for landing on snow. While engaged in bombing the station of Novo-Aleksyeevka an enemy machine was seen circling to gain height to attack. The bombing was finished at a height of 3000ft. and the enemy machine was still below at about 2,500ft. was then attacked after several bursts had been fired from our rear gun the Sopwith endeavoured to make off with his nose well down. We chased him and got into position for several more bursts from our Lewis gun from about 2,000ft. He was then at about 1,700ft. and immediately dived and landed about 2 miles SW of Novo-Aleksyeevka station in open country. Two men were seen to get out and run towards the station, no tracer ammunition was fired by the enemy.[1]

Also on 18 February, Captain Langley returned to Djankoi with the additional DH9 and a second bombing raid was carried out on A Flight at

A Sopwith 1½ Strutter of the type brought down on 18 February 1920 by Captain J. W. B. Grigson and Captain C. F. Gordon.

Djankoi. This time only two bombs were dropped: one failed to explode and the other hit a railway embankment and threw up some loose earth, causing very little damage.

It would seem that Captain Grigson's machine was the only serviceable one, as he and Gordon carried out the only sortie on 19 February, when an aircraft on the ground at Djimbuluk was bombed, with no hits being recorded. During the morning of 20 February, Grigson again bombed the railway station at Novo-Aleksyeevka. Two armoured trains and other rolling stock were hit. A second reconnaissance was carried out in the afternoon and three ships were found frozen into the Sea of Azov. Rolling stock on the rail lines was again bombed. The weather was too bad for flying on 21 February.

On 22 February, Major Collishaw made a reconnaissance over the Chongar peninsula with Captain Gordon. An armoured train was spotted and attacked with fourteen 20 lb bombs and 400 rounds of machine-gun fire. In his book, Collishaw claimed that while bombing the Red Army train his DH9 was hit by ground fire and the engine would not give full power. He managed to get back across the lines before making a forced landing twenty miles from the airfield at Djankoi. There had been a heavy fall of snow and he was able to taxi on the packed snow for the twenty miles back to base. The squadron diary, however, differs somewhat in the distance covered:

> Reconnaissance uncompleted owing to mist and clouds. Engine failed on return journey and machine was forced to land 3 miles North of Djankoi, an engine big end being broke.[2]

Collishaw may have been exaggerating slightly.

The weather conditions precluded any flying on 23, 24, or 25 February. On 26 February, Captain Breakey and Captain Langley carried out short test flights on two DH9s. Major Collishaw left Djankoi on 27 February, with Captain Gordon, and flew a DH9 to Ekaterinodar for Collishaw to have talks with Major Archer. One enemy aircraft tried to bomb the A Flight train on 27 February, but although two bombs were dropped they fell at least one mile wide. No other flying was possible for the rest of the month because of bad weather.

From 11 February to 8 March, Z Flight operated from the airfield at Ekaterinodar under the command of Lieutenant Ritchie. Flying RE8s, a small number of reconnaissances took place. Amongst the pilots attached to the flight were Lieutenants Wallace, Whitehead, Edward Fullford (Marion Aten claimed that Fullford was part of B Flight but this does not seem to have been the case), and Reid. The unrest amongst the Kuban

Cossacks continued to mount. General Holman sent a manifesto to the Kuban Cossacks in the name of the King. Lieutenant Ritchie carried out several flights across the Kuban area, dropping leaflets on the Cossack villages calling on them to rejoin their regiments. Holman had been made an honorary Cossack and he hoped the leaflets signed by himself would make a difference.

Captain Slatter, head of the RAF Kuban Group, had managed to get one DH9A into flying condition, and with Lieutenant Hesketh as his observer carried out a bombing raid on 17 February. This raid was on the airfield at Taganrog, which had been the main RAF base until a few weeks earlier. His combat report reads:

7/2/20 Captain Slatter. Lt. Hesketh. DH9A 9749 Objective Taganrog. Load 3x112lb bombs. Place Sea of Azov, Baltic Works and Taganrog Aerodrome. Very foggy. Sea of Azov is frozen over completely at Eastern end. There were no signs of activity on the aerodrome. The snow showed no wheel marks. 1st bomb fell near two aeroplane cases on the aerodrome. 2nd bomb fell on aerodrome just short of main shed. 3rd bomb fell alongside main buildings on the rail line. There was small train standing on N. side of works without an engine. A small party of men came out of shed on approach of aircraft.[3]

This particular aircraft (DH9A 9749) was apparently transferred to the Crimea Group by 4 March 1920.

Captain Anderson and C Flight were also at Ekaterinodar during February, as Anderson recorded:

Here, with aid of some hangars and some milder weather we managed to get several machines flying and were preparing to move up the line again when it was decided that the cause was hopeless and we were ordered to retreat to Novorossisk, where we arrived on the 4th March.[4]

It seems that even the redoubtable Anderson could not defy the collapsing situation and the prevailing conditions. The Kuban Group standing orders issued on 21 February included the following instruction:

All officers and ORs must be in the possession of a Rifle, Bayonet and 150 rounds of ammunition. These must in all cases be carried when travelling.[5]

The perilous state of affairs in the Kuban, with the entire White Army on the brink of collapse, was summed up in that order for the RAF men to carry rifles wherever they went. The Army tank school had moved to the Crimea, and during February most of the remaining tanks were also transported to the Crimea. At Helwan in Egypt, on 1 February, 47 Squadron was reformed by renumbering 206 Squadron.

NOTES

[1] National Archives, Grigson, J. W. B., combat report
[2] National Archives, 47 Squadron diary
[3] National Archives, Slatter, L. H., combat report
[4] National Archives, Anderson, W. F., War Experiences
[5] National Archives, Standing Orders Kuban Group

CHAPTER NINETEEN

MARCH 1920

The Red Army was poised for final victory in the Caucasus at the start of March 1920. Behind the White Army lines, large numbers of what became called the Green Guards were operating against what was left of Denikin's Army. These Green Guards were mainly composed of deserters from all the armies operating in the area. On two occasions, they were very nearly able to capture Novorossisk. Denikin was forced to withdraw a Don Army division from the front line in an effort to control the Green Guards. The Kuban Cossack politicians continued to make trouble for Denikin, and their troops continued to withdraw from the front line and return to their villages. Denikin attempted to withdraw behind the Kuban River and hold the west bank.

The Red Army entered Ekaterinodar on 18 March. Denikin's Army failed to blow the road and rail bridges over the Kuban River and the Red Army was soon across. The retreat continued to the port at Novorossisk. All the available Russian shipping and all the British ships in the Black Sea carried out a massive evacuation of White troops to the Crimea. At least 34,000 troops and some dependants were ferried across, but large numbers were left behind to surrender to the Red Army. In the Crimea, the White Army was still having no difficulty holding the Red Army at bay. By the end of the month, General Denikin had lost the confidence of his troops and after much discussion General Wrangel was invited to return and take command of what was left of the Armed Forces of South Russia.

A Flight continued to operate in the Crimea. The weather early in the month was poor, but Major Collishaw and Captain Gordon managed to fly back from Ekaterinodar on 3 March. Captain Breakey and Lieutenant Chubb made the first combat flight of the month on 7 March, when enemy transport and cavalry were bombed and machine-gunned. On the morning of 9 March, Collishaw carried out a reconnaissance and reported that the

British tanks being transported on a rail flatcar during the evacuation.

Red Army had advanced and occupied the town of Juschun. Grigson and Gordon also reported enemy cavalry and transport in the town of Juschun. They attacked these troops with bombs and machine-guns. Later in the day, they carried out a second flight and bombed a Red artillery battery and transport targets south of the town. Captain Breakey and Lieutenant Chubb reported that at least 1,000 enemy cavalry were north-west of Juschun and that 600 infantry were inside the town. These were attacked and the cavalry scattered. The squadron diary reads:

> The Volunteer Army by a brilliant counter attack drove the enemy out of Juschun and restored their position ultimately advancing a good number of versts. The enemy from subsequent reports suffered considerable casualties from aerial attack and their moral was certainly shaken by them.[1]

Three sorties were launched on the following day to continue the attack, but bad weather forced their early return. Flying was possible again on 12 March, and two sorties were carried out, with enemy troop and transport targets being bombed and machine-gunned.

Bad weather stopped flying until 17 March, when Captain Langley and Lieutenant Brockley bombed the railway station at Novo-Aleksyeevka. During the raid they were attacked by two enemy aircraft and shot one down, as recorded in their combat report:

> Combats in the Air. Squadron 47 [the pilots obviously still thought they were part of 47 Squadron]. Date 17/3/20. Type of Aeroplane DH9 2942. Time 3.5pm Armament 1 Vickers 1 Lewis. Locality Novo-Aleksyeevka. Pilot Captain M. J. Langley. Observer Lieut. T. W. Brockley. Height 4,000–5,000 feet. Result Driven down out of control. Remarks on Hostile Aircraft Nieuport single seater with powerful engine. Narrative. Two seater probable D. R. W. rear gun firing smoke tracer attacked from underneath while the other attacked from above. Two seater broke off engagement after 1 burst of 15 rounds at it. Nieuport pilot was evidently an experienced pilot, and made several determined attacks from all positions. As he was doing a heavy banked turn a burst of about 20 rounds was fired into him from the rear gun the tracers going right into him. He dropped into a vertical side slip for about 1,000 feet and then was seen to turn over into a vertical nose dive finally disappearing into the mist.[2]

Later on 17 March, Grigson and Gordon carried out a reconnaissance requested by the Russian staff. On the return flight, one of the big ends went on the engine and they were lucky to be able to return to Djankoi.

Langley and Brockley bombed infantry at Chongar on 18 March. Poor weather halted operations on 19 and 20 March, and the only flying carried out was a communications flight by Grigson, when he flew an Army Colonel Walsh to Theodosia and back to Djankoi. On 22 March, Langley and Brockley bombed the railway station at Djimbuluk and reported on the numbers of rolling stock in use on the Chongar Peninsula. The weather conditions again stopped flying until 28 March, when Grigson and Gordon carried out a reconnaissance of the front in the morning and reported things to be generally quiet. In addition, a group of cavalry and an artillery battery were bombed. In the afternoon, the same two attacked an armoured train north of Chongar. Several hits were obtained and the train was machine-gunned. These were the last flights carried out by A Flight.

The squadron diary for the rest of the month reads:

29/3/20. Orders received for detachment to proceed home via Theodosia. 30/3/20. 5 am Detachment train left Djankoi for Theodosia arriving at midday. 31/3/20. Detachment handed train to B.M.M. and embarked on H.M.T. Katoria at 4 pm for Constantinople via Sevastopol.[3]

Most of the flight personnel left on 31 March, though some of the senior officers left later.

Collishaw, in his book *Air Command* and in his log-book, claimed to have carried out at least seventeen sorties in the Crimea. This is probably more than the entire flight achieved. Records for only two flights by Collishaw can be found. He also stated that the aircraft were DH9As, but it seems reasonably certain that they were DH9s supplied by the Russians. The chronology and dates in his log-book for the retreat into the Crimea are wrong. This would seem to imply that the log-book was written up at a much later date and that he simply made some of it up.

In the Kuban, by early March, B and C Flights were in Novorossisk. Z Flight was still at Ekaterinodar to support what was left of Denikin's Army. On 4, 5, 6, and 7 March, Z Flight RE8s dropped propaganda leaflets on Kuban Cossack villages in an attempt to keep them in the fight. One flight was fired on from a village close to Ekaterinodar. On 7 March, Major Archer moved back to Novorossisk to take charge of the evacuation plans. Captain Slatter took command of Z Flight. At Novorossisk, sixty other ranks volunteered to continue to serve in south Russia, but the majority chose to be evacuated to Britain. On 13 March, the RAF evacuated Ekaterinodar. The train took three days to reach Novorossisk on 16 March. Marion Aten claims the RAF train was attacked en route, but there is no mention of this. In any case, Aten was already at Novorossisk and had been for some time. Lieutenant Ritchie summarised the withdrawal:

We retreated to the sea where our aircraft were burnt.[4]

Back in Britain, the strength of the British Military Mission in south Russia was given in the House of Commons by Churchill, on 2 March, as 394 officers and 1,529 other ranks, including 93 officers and 291 other ranks of the RAF. By 18 March, all the RAF personnel were in the cement works at Novorossisk. This was situated high on a bluff overlooking the port.

At Novorossisk, Major Archer attempted to save as much of the RAF stores as possible. There were 250 tons of RAF equipment stored on the docks at Novorossisk. This did not include the twenty-three aircraft in storage – ten RE8s, nine Avro 504s, and four DH9s. The RE8s were wrecked, along with the spares for the type, because it was thought the Russian dislike for the type meant they were unlikely to be used effectively. To save the remaining thirteen aircraft, they were handed over to the Russians, who claimed they could ship them to the Crimea. But this did not happen, and on 26 March these aircraft were also rendered unserviceable. It was done in a hurry, as Archer stated in his report:

> ...there being then not even time to unscrew the instruments from the dashboards.[5]

Marion Aten claims that tanks were used to crush brand-new aircraft in their crates on the docks, but no other sources mention this.

In late March, the 6th White Russian Air Force unit, the one that had been on the same airfield as the British units on the Kharkov front in December, was on an airstrip in Grozni. To escape the Red advance, they flew over the Caucasus Mountains into Georgia. The unit's four Sopwith Camels were taken into the Georgian air force. One of the pilots was Alexander Pishvanov, who later went to America and in the 1940s worked for Walt Disney. During the First World War, he had claimed five enemy aircraft shot down.

Most of the RAF personnel who had volunteered to serve in the Crimea sailed from Novorossisk on 24 March on board HMT *Baron Beck*. Archer stayed behind with a small party and the non-volunteers to finish the clearing-up. An attempt was made to help the Russian air force rescue as many of the aircraft they had been using as possible. It was thought that the Russians only managed to save around six DH9s and a small number of RE8s.

The situation in the town was utter chaos, as the defeated troops streamed in hoping for rescue. Major Jenks, who was with the Army in Novorossisk, wrote:

The docks at Novorossisk during the evacuation.

> Novorossisk was crammed with refugees from all over the Don. Not
> often can one have seen people dying of wounds, typhus, starvation,
> exposure, drowning or just plain despair all at the same time and place.
> Trying to control the rush to get away was heart breaking; once the
> crowd in their panic broke through our cordon and swarmed onto a
> small ship overturning it and all on board into the icy water.[6]

Thousands of bodies were found in the streets every morning. The Cossack
troops had arrived at Novorossisk with their horses; when they were told
that there was no room for the horses on the ships they shot them rather
than allow them to fall into the hands of the Reds. The docks became
littered with thousands of dead horses. General Milner, the commander of
the British Forces in the Black Sea, arrived in Novorossisk with a battalion
of the Royal Scots Fusiliers to oversee the withdrawal, but things were so
chaotic that little could be done. Two British tanks had been kept back
and they were used to cover the evacuation. Captain Anderson described
the scene in Novorossisk:

> We stayed there three weeks and I will never forget the terrible confusion
> and the appalling pitiful sights as the refugee ships sailed wives and families
> going and their men folk remaining to meet again heaven knew where.[7]

The British battleship *Emperor of India*. During the evacuation of Novorossisk, the *Emperor of India* bombarded Red Army troops waiting outside the port.

The British and French Navies had warships in the harbour. During the evacuation, the British battleship *Emperor of India* and the French cruiser *Waldeck Rousseau* opened fire on Budenny's forces waiting outside the port.

Two Sopwith Camels had been brought to Novorossisk on board the *Baron Beck* and they were assembled ready to fly in an emergency. The long, straight breakwater at the entrance to the harbour was the intended runway, but when the seaplane carrier HMS *Pegasus* arrived in the port the Camels were dismantled on 26 March and shipped out. The remainder of the RAF men were taken on board HMT *Hanover* on 26 March and the ship sailed at 23.00 hours. On 27 March, the Red Army entered Novorossisk and captured an enormous amount of British equipment that had not been destroyed. They also captured thousands of White Army troops who had not been able to get away.

The *Hanover* reached Theodosia in the Crimea on 27 March. Because of the situation, the plan for Anderson to take over A Flight was abandoned. The RAF presence in the Crimea was reduced to an advisory and training role. This reduced group was to comprise eighteen officers and thirty-five other ranks. Most of the RAF men left the Crimea on board SS *Katoria* on 31 March. Collishaw and Kinkead left in early April after clearing up the accounts for the units they had commanded. General Holman handed over command of the British Military Mission to General J. S. J. Percy and left the Crimea for Constantinople on 29 March with General Denikin.

NOTES

[1] National Archives, 47 Squadron diary
[2] National Archives, Langley, M. J., combat report
[3] National Archives, 47 Squadron diary
[4] National Archives, Ritchie, A. P., War Experiences
[5] National Archives, Archer, J. O., report on the evacuation of Novorossisk
[6] National Archives, Jenks, Major, War Experiences
[7] National Archives, Anderson, W. F., War Experiences

CHAPTER TWENTY

CONCLUSION

Wrangel had replaced Denikin to become the supreme commander on 4 April 1920. What was left of the Armed Forces of South Russia was concentrated in the Crimea. The Perekop Isthmus, connecting the Crimea to the mainland, is only five miles wide at its narrowest point. Wrangel was able to create trench lines across the isthmus to hold the Red Army at bay. There were about 35,000 troops left in the Crimea, and Wrangel mounted a major effort to re-equip and re-train the White forces. He tried to create a more disciplined force, as he blamed indiscipline, corruption, and looting for much of the misfortune that had befallen Denikin. On the political side, he also tried to create a viable consensus on the way forward and on the question of land for the people.

The British Military Mission had been reduced in size, but the British guaranteed to support Wrangel in the Crimea. Small amounts of military supplies, including tanks and aircraft, were delivered to the Crimea. The RAF contingent, under the command of Major Clemson, was only for advice and the limited provision of training. The full might of the Red Army was not immediately directed against the Crimea, as the Polish Army had opened a major assault against the Soviets. On 25 April, three Polish Armies attacked western Russia. At first, the Poles were successful, forcing the Red Army to move forces from south Russia to the new theatre.

The British government warned Wrangel against taking advantage of the weakness of the Soviet forces in south Russia and launching an attack on the mainland, but Wrangel ignored this warning and on 7 June 1920 the renamed Russian Army broke out of the Crimea and quickly captured the Taurida. On 11 June, the British withdrew the remaining Military Mission, including the RAF. Wrangel was told that Britain would now be neutral in the Civil War. But the French government continued to support Wrangel. To start with, the White advance was successful, but with only limited numbers of troops and equipment it soon ground to a halt. Wrangel was undoubtedly the best of the White generals in the south, but there was a limit to what even he could achieve.

By September, the Red Army had driven back the Poles and then been driven back again themselves. Both sides were keen to reach a settlement, and talks started in September. This released large numbers of troops to use against Wrangel. In October, the Russian Army was back to the Crimea. This time, the full might of the Red Army was directed against the Russian Army. Wrangel recognised the inevitable and took care to organise a full evacuation. He had heard the stories of the evacuation from Novorossisk and did not want this to happen again. By early November, the Red Army had broken through the Perekop Isthmus with heavy casualties. A major evacuation was mounted and by 16 November, 146,000 people had been lifted off and had crossed the Black Sea to Constantinople. The Russian Civil War in south Russia was over.

The reasons for the failure of the White Armies in south Russia were many and varied. General Denikin's Army was made up of a number of groups who had different views and aims. Denikin's view of 'one Russia indivisible' did not agree with the views of the Don, Kuban, or Terek Cossacks, or with the Ukrainians, who all wanted to create their own breakaway states. Many of the working classes in the White areas supported the Soviet state. When Denikin advanced towards Moscow he never had enough forces to control the land he had captured. The rear areas were in total chaos by December 1919. The corruption that followed the White Armies halted any attempts at logical organisation. After years of war and civil war, famine, and pestilence, the vast majority of the population just wanted peace at any price. Large numbers of people conscripted into the White Armies deserted. Although the same could also be said of the other side (two thirds of the troops conscripted into the Red Army deserted), at the end of the day, the government in Moscow had more men and resources. By late 1920, General Wrangel faced a Red Army with a paper strength of five million.

The British had played a major part in the fortunes of the Armed Forces of South Russia. The numbers of people involved were small, but the amounts of equipment supplied were enormous. 198,000 rifles of various types were supplied, along with 6,200 machine-guns and 500 million rounds of ammunition. Heavy equipment given to Denikin's troops included 1,120 artillery pieces, plus shells and at least seventy-four tanks. Hundreds of thousands of uniforms and boots were supplied. Over one million pairs of socks were lost at Novorossisk alone.

There is no really hard figure for the total of aircraft supplied. A number of aircraft that were being prepared for shipment were never sent after

Short 184 N9085 after it had been captured by the Reds in 1920.

the Army was forced to move to the Crimea. Also, aircraft that were supposed to have been sent never seem to have arrived. Other aircraft were scrapped on arrival, and six SE5As that were sent were never used, as the wrong propellers arrived with the aircraft. At least 100 RE8s were sent, with seventy-one being issued to the Russians. How much use was made of them is a different question. Counting the aircraft scrapped or never issued, at least 184 aircraft were received in south Russia; of these, at least 134 were issued to the Russians. The rest were either used by 47 Squadron or the Training Mission, or remained in storage. This figure does not include the aircraft used by 221 and 266 Squadrons. Only the RE8s and the Short 184s used by 266 Squadron were new aircraft; the rest were all second-hand ex-RAF stocks.

The RAF squadrons in south Russia were never very large, but they played a role out of all proportion to their size. They were the only really effective air units available to the Russians. Number 47 Squadron, operating on the Tsaritsin front, played a significant part in Wrangel's battles to hold onto the city. What the average members of the RAF thought they were doing in the middle of Russia is hard to judge. The British never really understood the situation in Russia or the issues involved. The average Russian was described as highly intelligent, cultured, and cosmopolitan, but also unreliable and utterly feckless. Much of the British aid vanished down a bottomless well of corruption, or was kept in storage at Novorossisk and never issued through inefficiency, only to fall into the hands of the Red Army.

Detail of picture on p. 116..

RAF PERSONNEL IN SOUTH RUSSIA

RAYMOND COLLISHAW

Although he is not as well remembered now as some other First World War pilots, Raymond Collishaw was one of the all-time great fighter pilots. He was born in Nanaimo, British Columbia, in 1893 and went to sea on leaving school. He served with the Canadian Fisheries Protection Service until he joined the Royal Naval Air Service in 1916. After learning to fly in England, he was posted to France to take part in the bombing campaign being mounted by the RNAS against Germany. While he was a member of 3 Wing, he flew a two-seat Sopwith 1½ Strutter on raids deep into Germany. During late 1916, he shot down two German fighters while flying Sopwith bombers. In February 1917, he was transferred to 3N Squadron, flying Sopwith Pup single-seat fighters. He shot down two German two-seaters before he was moved to 10N Squadron as a flight commander. This was a new squadron equipped with Sopwith Triplanes. Collishaw's flight became the famous 'Black Flight', with the cowlings and wheels of all the aircraft painted black. Each of the aircraft was given a name, starting with 'Black'; Collishaw's was 'Black Maria'. All the pilots in the flight became aces. By the time he left 10N Squadron, on 28 July 1917, Collishaw had shot down thirty-eight German aircraft. On 6 July 1917, he shot down six aircraft, the first pilot to claim six in one day.

The pictures of Collishaw show a slightly chubby, round, boyish face. But to belie this image, Collishaw became a complete killing machine. He returned to France in November as squadron leader of 13N Squadron, later 203 Squadron. Between then and September 1918, he raised his personal score to fifty-eight (possibly sixty-eight) German aircraft shot down. All the people who served with Collishaw who have written about the experience tell of a hard-living true leader of men. Ira Jones, who shot down forty German aircraft on the Western Front, served under Collishaw during the 1920s, and he later wrote of an occasion when Collishaw was a passenger in an aircraft that crashed in the desert:

> When near Quizilrobat the engine concked and they crashed. Not depressed for a moment, Collishaw, who is the famous Canadian air ace, said to David [Hughie David, the pilot who crashed] as he disentangled himself from the passenger cockpit: 'If we had some beer we could have a party.'[1]

After the end of the First World War, Collishaw was offered a permanent commission in the RAF and, after a period of leave in Canada, he was sent to command 47 Squadron in south Russia.

Collishaw remained in the RAF, and during 1940-41 he commanded 201 Group in Egypt and, later, 12 Group of Fighter Command. He retired in 1943 as an air vice marshal. After returning to Canada, he worked in the mining industry before he died in 1976. Collishaw was one of the RAF's great characters and fighting leaders.

Some of the claims that he made in his book *Air Command* about his time with 47 Squadron are hard to substantiate. Squadron records show that he carried out fewer combat sorties than he claimed. He stated that he flew seven combat sorties in one of B Flight's Camels between 7 and 10 October 1919: during these seven flights he claimed to have had three combats with enemy aircraft and to have shot one of them down, on 9 October. In each case, the enemy aircraft was an Albatross D-V. No mention of this type of enemy aircraft appears anywhere else in the RAF records for Russia. Furthermore, Collishaw is not shown as ever flying one of B Flight's aircraft and no mention of the shot-down aircraft can be found in squadron records. The idea that a squadron commander could shoot down an enemy aircraft and this not to be mentioned in the squadron records is not credible. In his log-book, Collishaw claimed that he was flying Camel B6396, though this aircraft was never listed as part of B Flight. In fact, records show that this aircraft was involved in a mid-air collision and was later broken up, on 12 November 1917, almost two years before Collishaw claimed he was flying it. Collishaw did not need to exaggerate: he was one of the great pilots.

SAMUEL MARCUS KINKEAD

Sam Kinkead was a South African, who was born in Johannesburg on 25 February 1897. He joined the RNAS in 1915. In 1916, he was with the Naval forces in the Dardanelles and was credited with shooting down three aircraft. He was later transferred to France, where he served in the

1st Naval Squadron and with 201 Squadron. By the end of the First World War, he had shot down thirty-two aircraft (possibly thirty-five). After he had returned from Russia, Kinkead again served with Collishaw in 30 Squadron. The squadron took part in several actions in support of Britain's imperial policy in the Middle East. As one of the best pilots in the RAF, Kinkead was chosen to be part of the famous Schneider Trophy team. He crashed into the Solent on 12 March 1928 while flying a Supermarine S5, and was killed.

JOHN OLIVER ANDREWS

Andrews was a regular Army officer before the First World War. He transferred to the RFC and was an observer with 5 Squadron in France. By 1916, he had received pilot training and was serving with 24 Squadron in France. At the end of the war, he was a major commanding 209 Squadron. His final score was twelve aircraft destroyed and twelve aircraft driven down. After serving in Russia, he received a permanent commission in the RAF, finally retiring with the rank of air vice marshal.

ROWAN HEYWOOD DALEY

Daley was born on 30 March 1898. He joined the RNAS and by 1817 he had trained as a pilot and was serving with the Home Defence Forces. He later served in France with the 10th Naval Squadron, being wounded while flying a Camel. By the end of the war, he had shot down three German aircraft. After serving in Russia with 47 Squadron, he received a permanent commission in the RAF but was killed in a mid-air collision in 1923.

LEONARD HORATIO SLATTER

Born at Durban, South Africa, on 8 December 1894, he joined the RNAS at the start of the First World War and served with an armoured car unit. By 1915, he was an observer with a Short seaplane unit operating in France. He was selected for pilot training and by 1917 he was flying a Sopwith 1½ Strutter on bombing missions. Later in the war, he claimed seven enemy aircraft destroyed while flying Sopwith Pups and Camels. After serving in 47 Squadron in Russia, he went on to command various squadrons during the inter-war years. He also served on the aircraft carrier

HMS *Courageous*. In 1937, he was promoted to group captain. This was followed by promotion to air commodore in 1940. He was AOC in Iraq and during the campaigns in Abyssinia and Eritrea. In late 1941, he was in command of 201 Group in Egypt. He was transferred back to Britain in 1943 to command 15 Group in Coastal Command. By 1945, he was the chief of Coastal Command, with the rank of air marshal. He died in 1961.

ARTHUR CLINTON MAUND

Maund was born in Paddington on 13 December 1891. At the start of the First World War he was in Canada and enlisted in the Canadian infantry. In March 1916, he transferred to the RFC as an observer with 8 Squadron. After flying training, he served as a pilot with 7 Squadron. He served with the Russian mission on the Galician front in 1917, and with the North Russian Expeditionary Force at Archangel in 1918. A permanent commission was granted to him in 1920, with the rank of squadron leader. During the 1920s and 1930s he served at various RAF posts and was promoted to air marshal in 1939. He died in 1942.

WILLIAM ELLIOT

Elliot was born in 1896 and joined the Army in 1914. It was not until 1917 that he transferred to the RFC. He was posted to Palestine to join 142 Squadron in March 1918. The squadron had an intensely busy time in the campaign in Palestine, from the operations around El Salt until the fall of Damascus. After serving with 47 Squadron, he stayed in the RAF. By 1937, he was the assistant secretary (air) to the Committee of Imperial Defence. During the Second World War, he held various commands, including a night fighter base, and also became chief of the Balkan Air Force. After the war, he led Fighter Command and retired as an air chief marshal. He died in 1971.

RALPH SORLEY

Sorley was born on 9 January 1898 at Hornsey, Middlesex. He joined the RNAS in 1914, and in 1916 was granted a commission; he transferred to the RAF in 1918. That same year, he was awarded the DSC for the day and night bombing of the *Breslau* and *Goeben*. After serving with

221 Squadron in south Russia, he was in 6 Squadron in Mesopotamia from 1920 to 1922. He then served with 14 Squadron in Palestine until 1924. Most of the rest of his career in the RAF was spent on the technical side, with spells commanding various bases. He also played a part in the establishment of the requirement for eight machine-guns as the armament for the Spitfire and Hurricane.

In 1941, Sorley was appointed assistant chief of air staff (technical requirements). He became controller of research and development at the Ministry of Aircraft Production in 1943 and was a member of the Air Council. Later, he was commander of the Technical Training Command until he retired as an air marshal in 1948. When he left the RAF, he joined DeHavilland Propellers Ltd and became the managing director.

CHRISTOPHER NEIL HOPE BILNEY

Bilney was born at Weybridge, Surrey, in October 1898, and was educated at Tonbridge School. He was commissioned in the RNAS in 1917. His first service was flying patrols over the North Sea in Short floatplanes. In 1918, he was transferred to the east Mediterranean, still flying seaplanes. After serving with 266 Squadron in south Russia, he was given a permanent commission in the RAF.

By 1939, Bilney was commander of the Aeroplane and Armaments Experimental Establishment. He was later in the Directorate of Armament Development. In 1942, he was vice president of the Ordinance Board. He moved to become Bomber Command's ordinance officer in 1944. When he retired in the 1950s, he was an air vice marshal.

MARION HUGHES ATEN

Aten was born in Amarillo, Texas, on 22 November 1894. His father was a famous Texas Ranger, who moved to California and started the 8 N Bar ranch in the Imperial Valley. Aten was commissioned in the RAF on 24 April 1918. He obtained his RAF flying certificate on 12 November 1918, the day after the Armistice. He volunteered to serve with 47 Squadron in south Russia and left the Crimea in 1920. In the early 1920s, he served in the Middle East and later worked with a training organisation stationed in England. He resigned his commission in 1927 and went back to California to run his father's ranch. In 1961, he published the story of his time in Russia under the title of *Last Train Over Rostov Bridge*, co-written with Arthur Orrmont. Aten died in 1961.

Aten's book has been responsible for more myths about 47 Squadron than any other, and should be viewed as semi-fictional. He claimed he was a captain, but he was never a captain or acting captain and was still a lieutenant when he retired in 1927. He also claimed that he fought in the First World War, in Collishaw's 203 Squadron, though he was never in 203 Squadron and did not receive his pilot's wings until the war was over. Among the other things he claimed was that he arrived in Russia in March 1919. This was before any 47 Squadron personnel arrived; it was only on 19 August that he reported for duty with 47 Squadron.

Aten was part of B Flight, commanded by Sam Kinkead. This unit did not go up to the front line until 28 September, but Aten claimed to have shot down five Russian aircraft by that date. In fact, no record can be found for any aircraft shot down by Aten. One of the aircraft that he claimed to have shot down in August was a black Fokker Triplane. This was supposed to have been flown by the leading Red air force pilot in south Russia, who had shot down twelve White air force aircraft. None of this ever happened. Because books dealing with this period are few, Aten's book has been taken as the truth by a generation of writers. The black Fokker Triplane has appeared in at least a dozen histories, one published as late as 2001. Aten also claimed that the other members of B Flight shot down a considerable number of enemy aircraft; this is not true either. The numbers of Red air force aircraft in the area was never very large. Only three aircraft were claimed as shot down by B Flight, two by Kinkead and one by Burns-Thomson.

Even the title of Aten's book is incorrect, as his train never made it across Rostov Bridge. He claimed to have been in Ekaterinodar in March 1920 when General Holman made an appeal for volunteers to stay and cover the retreat, but he had been in Novorossisk since January 1920. Aten was awarded a DFC for his exploits in Russia and he did take part in a number of ground attack sorties, but the citation for his medal says that it was for his actions on 27 October 1919. Squadron records show that no flying took place on this day because of bad weather. Having made these criticisms, his book does give a feel for the conditions in Russia during this period.

A. H. HESKETH

Born in London in July 1899, Hesketh joined the Army in 1917, was transferred to the RFC as a cadet in 1918, and was commissioned in the RAF in the same year . In 1920, he was awarded the DFC for services in south Russia. He retired from the air force as an air vice marshal.

WALTER FRASER ANDERSON

Anderson was born at Ryde on the Isle of Wight in 1890. His father, who was a minister, moved to Toronto in Canada while Anderson was a child. At the start of the First World War, he joined the Canadian Army and was sent overseas on 28 March 1915. Later, on 25 February 1916, he transferred to the RFC. While serving with 42 Squadron, he was wounded on 29 August 1916. He returned to serve in France with 9 Squadron between 14 September and 3 December 1917. Promoted to flight lieutenant, he served with 217 Squadron until the end of the war.

After serving with 47 Squadron in Russia, Anderson was given a permanent commission and stayed with the RAF until 1927. He worked for British Airways until he was killed in a crash in September 1936. After taking off from Gatwick, while flying a DH86 on the night mail run to Germany, he seems to have tried to turn back to the runway but lost height and crashed into a tree.

NOTES

[1] Jones, Ira, *An Air Fighter's Scrapbook*, Greenhill Books, London, 1990, page 171

Detail of picture on p. 172.

THE AIRCRAFT USED IN SOUTH RUSSIA

RE8

Length: 27 ft 10 in. *Span:* (upper wing) 42 ft 8 in; (lower wing) 32 ft 7 in. *Height:* 10 ft 10 in.
Wing area: 377 sq. ft. *Wing loading:* 7.6 lb/sq. ft.
Engine: one 150 hp RAF 4a 12-cylinder Vee piston engine. *Maximum speed:* 102 mph.
Service ceiling: 13,500 ft. *Weights:* (empty) 1,800 lbs; (loaded) 2,896 lbs.
Endurance: 4.5 hours. *Armament:* one Vickers fixed forward-firing machine-gun and one Lewis gun on a Scarff ring in rear cockpit; 250 lbs bomb load.

The RE8 was introduced in late 1916 as a two-seat reconnaissance and artillery spotting aircraft. It was never a popular aircraft and had to be withdrawn soon after its introduction after a series of crashes. The tail section was redesigned and the aircraft reintroduced. In general, it was a very stable aircraft but slow to manoeuvre and a sitting duck for the newer German types. By the time production ceased, over 4,000 had been produced and well over 2,000 served on the Western Front, equipping most of the Army co-operation squadrons.

The main reason the RE8 was sent to Russia was that the new aircraft were available to be sent in quantity immediately. The Russians had constant difficulties with the RE8 and in the end refused to use them. A number of crashes took place, leading to accusations by the Russians that the British were getting rid of condemned aircraft and the accusation by the British that the Russians were incompetent. The RE8 was perhaps not the best aircraft to have sent to Russia. The aircraft pictured above is shown in Red air force markings and is one of the RE8s captured at Taganrog.

RE8, pictured at Taganrog.

DH9 number D2854, pictured on the ground at Petrovsk.

DH9

Length: 30 ft 9 in. *Span:* 42 ft 6 in. *Height:* 11 ft 7 in.
Wing area: 436 sq. ft. *Wing loading:* 8.4 lb/sq. ft.
Engine: one 230 hp Sidney Puma. *Maximum speed:* 111.5 mph.
Service ceiling: 17,500 ft. *Weights:* (empty) 2,300 lbs; (loaded) 3,670 lbs.
Endurance: 4.5 hours. *Armament:* one Vickers forward-firing machine-gun and one or two Lewis guns in rear cockpit; up to 460 lbs bomb load.

The DH9, built by De Havilland, was essentially a redesign of the successful DH4. But the DH9 ended up slower and less manoeuvrable than the aircraft it was replacing. On the plus side, the pilot and observer were now closer together for easier communications, and a heavier bomb load than the DH4 could be carried. The original engine for the DH9 was the 200 hp BPH, but this was chronically unreliable, leading to the loss of many aircraft in France. Over 2,000 were built and they were responsible for a large percentage of the bombs dropped on Germany in the last year of the First World War.

All the DH9s used in Russia were second-hand and were sent from RAF stocks in the Middle East. The Puma engine was more reliable than the original BHP, and the Russians much preferred the DH9 to the RE8.

DH9A

Length: 30 ft 3 in. *Span:* 45 ft 11 in. *Height:* 11 ft 4 in.
Wing area: 493 sq. ft. *Wing loading:* 9.5 lb/sq. ft.
Engine: one 400 hp Liberty. *Maximum speed:* 114 mph.
Service ceiling: 16,500 ft. *Weights:* (empty) 2,695 lbs; (loaded) 4,645 lbs.
Endurance: 5.75 hours. *Armament:* one Vickers forward-firing machine-gun and one or two Lewis guns on Scarff ring in rear cockpit; bomb load of up to 660 lbs.

The DH9A was a further development of the DH9, with increased wing span and the American Liberty engine. This gave the DH9A a longer range and a larger bomb load. The Liberty engine was efficient and reliable, and the DH9A served with RAF squadrons for many years after the end of the First World War. Number 221 Squadron was re-equipped with the DH9A and passed on its DH9s to the White Russian squadrons. Using the DH9A from Petrovsk to bomb Astrakhan meant that the intermediate airfield at Chechen Island was no longer needed because of the aircraft's extra range.

A DH9A photographed on the ground at Petrovsk airfield.

A Flight of 47 Squadron was equipped with the DH9A while it was operating from Beketovka. This was a success while the flight was stationed at one place, and a large number of attacks on the Russian ships on the Volga took place. But when the squadron was on the move the more complex DH9A required an extra train to carry the necessary spares and equipment. A Flight's aircraft were wrecked during the evacuation of Tagenrog. Like the DH9s, all the DH9As used in Russia were second-hand aircraft.

SOPWITH CAMEL

Length: 19 ft 6 in. *Span:* 28 ft. *Height:* 9 ft.
Wing area: 231 sq. ft. *Wing loading:* 6.4 lb/sq. ft.
Engine: one 130 hp Clerget Rotary. *Maximum speed:* 115 mph.
Service ceiling: 19,000 ft. *Weights:* (empty) 929 lbs; (loaded) 1,453 lbs.
Endurance: 2.5 hours. *Armament:* two forward-firing Vickers machine-guns; four 25 lb Cooper Bombs.

The Camel had the distinction of shooting down more aircraft during the First World War than any other fighter aircraft. First introduced into service in June 1917, the Camel was a highly manoeuvrable aircraft. But this manoeuvrability was bought at the cost of stability and for

Captain Samuel Kinkead, standing next to his Sopwith Camel at Beketovka. The markings on the Camel are those of the Kuban air force.

inexperienced pilots the Camel was something of a handful. Large numbers of Allied pilots were killed after losing control of the Camel. In the hands of an experienced pilot like Sam Kinkead, the Camel was a formidable opponent.

A number of different engine types were employed in the Camel, but the ones used by 47 Squadron were Clerget-engined. One Bentley-engined Camel was taken to Petrovsk with 221 Squadron. Camels were also supplied to the White Russians and at least one Squadron, the 6th Don Squadron, used the type. All the Camels were alleged to have been destroyed during the evacuation, but there are photographs of at least one Camel in Red air force colours.

NIEUPORT 17

Length: 19 ft 7 in. *Span:* 27 ft. *Height:* 8 ft.
Wing area: 160 sq. ft. *Wing loading:* 7.7 lb/sq. ft.
Engine: one 110 hp Le Rhone rotary engine. *Maximum speed:* 106 mph.
Service ceiling: 16,500 ft. *Weights:* (empty) 825 lbs; (loaded) 1,235 lbs.
Endurance: 2.25 hours. *Armament:* one forward-firing Vickers machine-gun.

Nieuports of the 1st Kuban Squadron, pictured at Beketovka.

The Nieuport 17 was introduced into French service during 1915 and played a major part in restoring the balance against the German Fokker. Many of the Allied aces started their careers flying Nieuport types, including Ball and Bishop. It was a light, manoeuvrable aircraft with a good speed and climb rate for the conditions when it was introduced. One fault of the aircraft, because of its light weight, was a tendency to lose the top wing in steep dives. France manufactured thousands of Nieuports and the type was used by France, Britain, Italy, Belgium, and America, as well as Russia.

Both the White and the Red air forces used the Nieuport. Large numbers had been imported into Russia and it was also built in Russia under licence.

Although it had been an effective aircraft, the Nieuport was probably past its best by 1919, but the small numbers of aircraft available during the Russian Civil War meant that it was still a useful aircraft.

THE BRITISH MILITARY MISSION TO SOUTH RUSSIA COMMAND STRUCTURE

COMMANDING OFFICERS

General F. C. Poole, Nov. 1918-Feb. 1919; General Briggs, Feb. 1919-June 1919; General H. C. Holman, June 1919-Feb. 1920; General Payne, Feb.1920-June 1920.

Commanding Officers RAF in South Russia

Lieutenant-Colonel A. C. Maund, May 1919-Jan. 1920; Major J. O. Archer, Jan. 1920-April 1920; Major A. W. Clemson, April 1920-June 1920.

Commanding Officer 62 Wing

Lieutenant-Colonel F. W. Bowhill, Jan. 1919-Aug. 1919.

Commanding Officers 221 Squadron

Major J. O. Andrews, Dec.1918-May 1919; Major De Ville, May 1919-June 1919; Lieutenant-Colonel Gordon, June 1919-Aug. 1919.

Commanding Officer 266 Squadron

Captain J. A. Sadler, Feb. 1919-Aug. 1919.

Commanding Officer A Flight 17 Squadron

Captain A. D. Makins, Jan. 1919-Nov. 1919.

Commanding Officers 47 Squadron ('A Detachment' after Oct. 1919)

Captain S. G. Frogley, June 1919; Major R. Collishaw, June 1919-March 1920. **Commanding Officer A Flight 47 Squadron**

Captain L. H. Slatter, Oct. 1919-Dec. 1919.

Commanding Officer B Flight 47 Squadron

Captain S. Kinkead, Sept 1919-March 1920.

Commanding Officers C Flight 47 Squadron

Captain H. G. Davies, May 1919-July 1919; Captain S. G. Frogley, July 1919-Nov. 1919; Captain W. F. Anderson, Nov. 1919-March 1920.

Commanding Officers Z Flight

Major J. O. Archer, Nov. 1919-Jan. 1920; Captain A. P. Ritchie, Feb. 1920-

March 1920. **Commanding Officer Crimea Group**

Major R. Collishaw, Jan. 1920-March 1920.

Commanding Officer Kuban Group

Major L. H. Slatter, Jan. 1920-March 1920.

Commanding Officers Training Mission

Major L. P. Paine, May 1919-July 1919; Major J. O. Archer, July 1919-Nov. 1919.

Commanding Officer RAF Air Park Novorossisk

Captain A. W. Clemson, Sept. 1919-March 1920.

BIBLIOGRAPHY

Aten, M. H., *Last Train Over Rostov Bridge*, Cassell, London, 1961.

Bechhofer, C. E., *In Denikin's Army*, 1921.

Boyd, Alexander, *The Soviet Air Force*, Macdonald and Jane's, London, 1977.

Butt, V. P., *The Russian Civil War*, Macmillan Press Ltd, London, 1996.

Collishaw, Raymond, *Air Command*, William Kimber, London, 1970.

Cronin, Dick, *Royal Navy Shipboard Aircraft Developments*, Air-Britain Publications, 1990.

Denikin, A. I., *The White Army*, Ian Faulkner Publishing, Cambridge, 1992.

Fowler, Simon, *RAF Records in the PRO*, PRO Publications, London, 1994.

Dobson, Christopher and Miller, John, *The Day We Almost Bombed Moscow*, Hodder and Stoughton, London, 1986.

Hodgson, John Ernest, *With Denikin's Armies*, Lincoln Williams, London, 1932.

Jackson, Robert, *At War With The Bolsheviks*, Tandem, London, 1972.

Jane's Fighting Aircraft Of World War One, Studio Editions, London, 1990.

Jones, H. A., *Over the Balkans and South Russia*, 1923.

Jones, Ira, *An Air Fighter's Scrapbook*, Greenhill Books, London, 1990.

Khvostov, Mikhail and Karachtchouk, Andrei, *The Russian Civil War: The Red Army*, Osprey, London, 1996.

Khvostov, Mikhail and Karachtchouk, Andrei, *The Russian Civil War: The White Armies*, Osprey, London, 1997.

Lincoln, W. Bruce, *Red Victory*, De Capo Press, New York, 1999.

Maudsley, Evan, *The Russian Civil War*, Birlinn, Edinburgh, 2000.

Riaboff, Alexander, *Gatchina Days*, Smithsonian Institute Press, Washington, 1986. Seaton, Albert, *Stalin*, Combined Publishing, Pennsylvania, 1998.

Silverlight, John, *The Victors' Dilemma*, Barrie and Jenkins Ltd, London, 1970. Sturtivant, Ray and Page, Gordon, *The D.H. 4/D.H. 9 File*, Air-Britain Publications, 1999.

Sturtivant, Ray and Page, Gordon, *The Camel File*, Air-Britain Publications, 1993. Williamson, H. N. H., *Farewell to the Don*, 1970.

Wrangel, Alexis, *General Wrangel*, Leo Cooper, London, 1987.

Wrangel, Petr, *The Memoirs of General Wrangel*, Williams and Northgate Ltd, London, 1929.

Most of the records relating to the RAF in south Russia are in the National Archives at Kew. Other records are in the National Army Museum in Chelsea, the Maritime Museum in Greenwich, the RAF Museum in Hendon, and the British Library in the Euston Road.

INDEX

Also available from Amberley Publishing

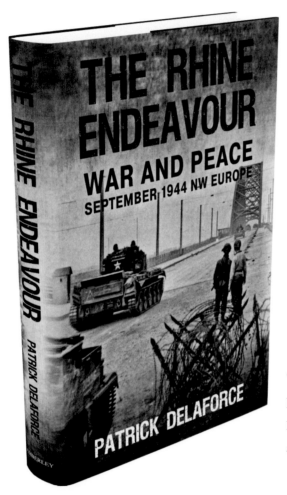

Also available from Amberley Publishing

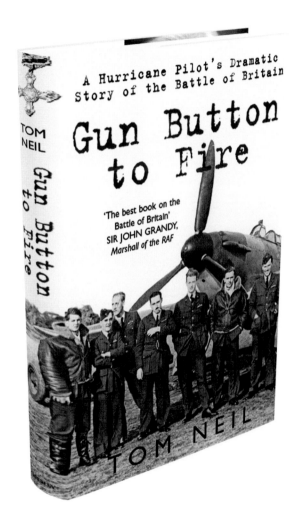

Gun Button to Fire
Tom Neil
ISBN: 978-1-84868-848-3
£20.00 HB

Available from all good bookshops, or order direct
from our website www.amberleybooks.com

Also available from Amberley Publishing

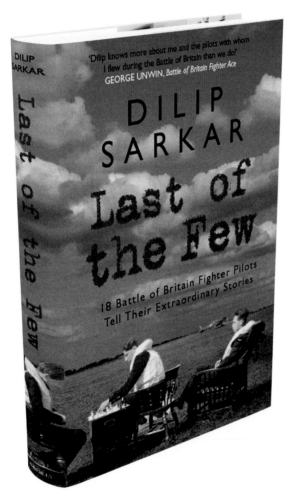

Last of the Few
Dilip Sarkar
ISBN: 978-1-84868-435-5
£20.00 HB

Available from all good bookshops, or order direct
from our website www.amberleybooks.com